INSIDE
Sacramento

The most interesting neighborhood places
in America's farm-to-fork capital

CECILY HASTINGS

INSIDE PUBLICATIONS

PUBLISHED BY INSIDE PUBLICATIONS

3104 O Street #120
Sacramento, CA 95816
Visit insidesacramento.com

Book design by Cecily Hastings, Brian Burch and Daniel Nardinelli

Library of Congress Cataloging-in-Publication data is available upon request.

Every effort was made to ensure the accuracy of the information in this book at press time.
However, certain details are subject to change. The publisher cannot accept responsibility for
any consequences arising from the use of this book.

Printed and bound in China
ISBN 978-1-945174-49-0
First Edition

This book is dedicated to my mother, Virginia Hayward, who helped publish
the first book on her small town's history in 1976. Her love of community
and spirit of volunteerism remain with me every day of my life.

Cecily Hastings

INTRODUCTION

Sacramento is known as America's Farm-to-Fork Capital. No other major American city is more centrally located amid so many small, family-owned farms, ranches and vineyards—all producing year-round in our ideal Mediterranean climate. Sacramento adopted the Farm-to-Fork Capital designation through the efforts of civic and business leaders who wanted to sing the praises of our local food-growing and food-making experience.

Sacramento is also home to one of the largest farmers markets in the state: the famed Sunday farmers market downtown, an exciting marketplace of fruits, vegetables, meat, fish, flowers and artisanal products. In Sacramento, some 40 other farmers markets attract tens of thousands of people each week seeking the farm-to-fork experience.

Sacramento celebrates farm-to-fork culture each September with a festival and other events capped by a gala dinner, at which hundreds of diners enjoy a locally sourced meal on the magnificent Tower Bridge. Guests are treated to a feast highlighting the delicious collaboration between the Sacramento region's farmers and chefs. The honored chefs selected to create the dinner are given a special green logo on their restaurant's page in this book.

But Sacramento doesn't always get the respect it deserves. Even though it is the state capital, it's often overshadowed by its larger and louder regional neighbors.

The discovery of gold in the Sacramento Valley in early 1848 sparked the historic Gold Rush. But in recent years, another rush has occurred: the development of the city's many diverse neighborhoods. People are attracted to these neighborhoods by the sheer number of interesting shops, restaurants, cafés and other commercial establishments. In addition, the new Golden 1 Center downtown has encouraged dozens of new developments that enrich the central city and beyond, bringing people from all over to dine, shop, explore and be entertained.

This book is a curated collection of Sacramento's most interesting places. It's designed to give readers an insider's glimpse into the unique and exceptional Sacramento neighborhood experience. It's not meant just for people who live in Sacramento, but also for visitors from all over the country who come on business or vacation or are considering moving here. The eight neighborhoods profiled in this book are among the city's most pleasant to visit on foot and by bike.

Sacramento is perfect for raising families, so we have indicated the places that especially welcome them.

This book was lovingly crafted as a guide to the delightful locally owned places we know about from living here and publishing neighborhood newsmagazines for the past two decades. Find yourself in Sacramento!

—Cecily Hastings

LC Studio Tutto, the art and design team of Sofia Lacin and Hennessy Christophel, recently completed the 70,000-square-foot "Bright Underbelly" mural at the Sunday farmers market location as an homage to the City of Trees.

INSIDE *Downtown*

Farm-to-fork culture comes alive at the Sunday farmers market in Southside Park; nearby is the magnificent state house in Capitol Park, our city's botanical garden, also home to the International World Peace Rose Garden.

Entertainment and dining options abound at local performance venues and at dozens of historic and new restaurants. Smaller historic residential neighborhoods including Southside Park and Alkali Flats are among the city's oldest and have an interesting collection of vintage homes.

Marvel at the Crocker Art Museum's galleries, filled with some of the finest historic and contemporary artwork in the West.

The new Golden 1 Center is bringing exciting new development, housing and life to our city core.

ANDY'S CANDY APOTHECARY

Glass jars sparkle with sweet treats along the shelves of Andy's Candy Apothecary, a nostalgic downtown wonderland for every candy aficionado. Open since 2013, the sweet shop is a magical place realized by owner Andy Paul, whose victory in Sacramento's first-ever Calling All Dreamers contest provided support to open the Apothecary. Paul won business services, rent and construction expenses. He transformed the opportunity into the candy store of his dreams. Today, Paul is Sacramento's resident candy expert. He's delighted to unravel the mysteries of sweets and can explain why all candy bars are not created equal, or how some Swedish fish are better than others. As a youngster, Paul spent allowance money and cash from his newspaper route on penny sweets and drugstore candy bars. These days, his business provides the world's finest sugary confections to customers of all ages.

1012 9th Street
916.905.4115
andyscandystore.com

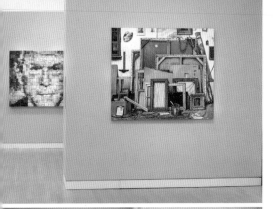

CROCKER ART MUSEUM

California art, works on paper, European art, international ceramics, photography, Asian art, African and Oceanic art and more—such is the diverse beauty awaiting discovery at the Crocker Art Museum. As the oldest public art museum in the West, the Crocker fulfills its cultural mission with expansive galleries and educational facilities that delight all ages. Built as a family mansion in 1885 by Edwin B. Crocker, the museum elevated its status as a regional destination in 2010 with the new Teel Family Pavilion. Ten years in the creation, the Pavilion adds 125,000 square feet to Crocker's historic mansion. The expansion more than tripled the museum's size and gave the Crocker dedicated gallery spaces for all collecting areas. The historic wing's first floor serves as the Education Center, which includes four studio classrooms, space for student and community exhibits, the expanded Gerald Hansen Library, the Art Education Resource Room and Tot Land. Traveling exhibitions—Andy Warhol, Edward Hopper and Norman Rockwell were favorites—join the Crocker's beautiful

collections. And the Crocker's Museum Store is the downtown destination for stylish, artistically inspired gifts and one-of-a-kind designs. Purchases support the museum's exhibits and programs. The Crocker Café serves snacks all day and offers counter service at lunch. Museum admission is not required to enjoy the café, elegant lobby, patio setting and store.

216 O Street
916.808.7000
crockerartmuseum.org

ALLSPICERY

A world of spice can be found in one location at Sacramento's ultimate culinary specialty shop. Allspicery is exactly what the name suggests—a place where the world's most difficult-to-find spices present themselves for adventurous chefs, both home-style and professional. The winner of the 2015 Downtown Sacramento Foundation's third annual Calling All Dreamers competition—where local hopefuls submit business plans to be considered for monetary awards that help make their retail dreams a reality—Allspicery is the vision of Heather Wong. A culinary enthusiast who had become frustrated with the scarcity of ethnic spices in Sacramento, Wong decided to take matters into her own hands and make global spices available to the community. An avid traveler, Wong was determined to deliver the flavors of the world to her adopted hometown. In the quaint Allspicery shop, chefs can experiment from among about 300 spices, most of which have been impossible to obtain at traditional retail outlets in Sacramento. Clients can purchase spices whole or have them freshly ground by Wong in-house to flavor special or daily dishes.

1125 11th Street
916.905.7948
allspicery.com

ESQUIRE GRILL

Elegant décor, soft lighting, rich mahogany wood floors and walls, and high-backed banquettes of tufted black leather make the Esquire Grill the perfect setting for political power lunches and dinner before the theater. Located at the bustling corner of 13th and K Streets, the Esquire Grill is surrounded by the Sacramento Convention Center, Community Center Theater, Esquire IMAX theater and the Hyatt Regency and Sheraton Grand hotels. With the State Capitol two blocks away, Esquire Grill serves as the town's top spot for celebrity sightings. Arnold Schwarzenegger was a regular as governor and a constellation of stars from Clint Eastwood to Gwyneth Paltrow have dropped by for lunch. The seasonal menu showcases classic dishes like the Dungeness crab and shrimp Louie salad. The ahi tuna burger is a favorite among legislators and lobbyists, served with spicy soy mayonnaise, pickled ginger, red onion and daikon sprouts. Grilled New York steak or a half-pound Angus burger will tempt heartier diners. Esquire Grill has a full bar and an extensive California wine list. Another fine touch from this restaurant is a well-seasoned wait staff, sure to please.

1213 K Street
916.448.8900
paragarys.com

HOCK FARM CRAFT & PROVISIONS

John Sutter began Northern California's first large-scale agricultural settlement on the Feather River in 1841 and called his land Hock Farm. In homage to Sutter's bountiful ranch, Hock Farm Craft & Provisions celebrates the Sacramento Valley's legacy of fresh fruits and vegetables and focuses on farm-to-fork dining with a menu that changes often while capitalizing on produce from local farms. The design is a modern interpretation of rustic styles from the mid-19th century, with a gleaming poured-concrete floor and the custom-made solid Douglas fir "California" table crafted in the shape of our golden state. Local and regional fabricators and artisans like 12M Design and Reclamation Art + Furniture gave Hock Farm its distinctive look. The menu is pure California—a mix of local and European—with highlights that include Di Stefano burrata and the grilled Romaine entrée salad with Creekstone flat iron steak, frisée, radicchio, shaved radish and Nantes carrot in a creamy buttermilk dressing. Penne with Dixon lamb ragu is served in an organic tomato sauce with Pecorino, hot pepper and crispy eggplant. The extensive craft bar featuring classic cocktails reimagined with local, fresh ingredients completes the delicious experience.

1415 L Street
916.440.8888
paragarys.com

CAFETERIA 15L

Reminiscent of the classic American lunch counter spiced with a millennial flavor, Cafeteria 15L serves an eclectic array of comfort food that foodies appreciate. Lunch favorites include elevated delicacies such as truffle tater tots, French fries served in faux newsprint, macaroni and cheese, Caesar salad, meatloaf and the enduringly popular French dip sandwich, tossed back with a glass of plantation iced tea or house-made fruit punch. Dinner resolves any cravings for buttermilk fried chicken strips or onion strings, chicken and waffles or braised beef short ribs served with mushroom risotto. And there's brunch, where chocolate banana waffles, brioche French toast, inventive skillets and benedicts indulge all appetites. Designed by the interior artists who brought the look of the W Hotels chain to the world, Cafeteria 15L features two plush outdoor patios, a comfortable lounge space and large areas dedicated to private and semi-private dining, plus the main dining room. Reclaimed woods, industrial light fixtures and an array of mixed and matched chairs create an atmosphere whimsical and cozy. The familiar cafeteria has never looked cooler—another success story from the local Wong family of restaurants, led by brothers Mason, Curtis and Alan Wong.

1116 15th Street
916.492.1960
cafeteria15l.com

CORNFLOWER CREAMERY

Farm-to-scoop artisanal ice cream flavors created by adventurous culinary entrepreneur Cynthia Broughton make Cornflower Creamery a unique downtown experience. Flavors include Beer & Pretzels, conjured from Oak Park Brewing Company's Imperial Stout with dark chocolate and chocolate-covered pretzels. Lemon Olive Oil is made with California Olive Ranch olive oil and locally grown lemons. The creamery, located adjacent to Capitol Park,

offers treats far beyond the galaxy of predictable ice cream. And Broughton is committed to building community relationships with fellow local businesses and organizations. For example, the Bedtime Story flavor—featuring caramel and graham crackers—was created for the Sacramento Public Library Children's Reading Hour. Cornflower Creamery features vegan and dairy-free options and sandwiches and salads made from scratch with organic ingredients, plus craft colas. The brightly lighted dining room highlights displays of cow paintings commissioned by local artists.

1013 L Street
916.970.5411
cornflowercreamery.com

24

DOWNTOWN & VINE

Expanding the Sacramento community's exposure to unique wines from California and around the globe is the mission of Downtown & Vine. With two wine clubs for customers and servings offered in tasting flights, glasses or by the bottle, Downtown & Vine provides the opportunity and atmosphere to taste and compare the region's best wines, craft beers and international labels. The downtown K Street location, just a block from the Community Center Theater, provides an inviting atmosphere for after-work gatherings. The kitchen creates masterful small plates—tapas, flatbreads and charcuterie—to enhance the vibe. Downtown & Vine's retail selection is maintained by a knowledgeable staff and carries a vast selection of wine and beer to take home or send as gifts. The store can ship to 42 states, making long-distance gift shopping simple.

1200 K Street, Suite 8
916.228.4518
downtownandvine.com

DE VERE'S IRISH PUB

A corner of Ireland's capital has been transported 6,000 miles to create this lively downtown pub. The deVere White family comes from a long line of pub owners who emigrated from Dublin to the U.S. After settling in Sacramento, the family decided to reestablish their hometown experience, including 20-ounce pints of beer and lovingly poured Guinness Stout. The family contracted with Irish craftsmen to design and build each of the pub's fixtures and furnishings. The pieces were shipped from Ireland and reassembled in Sacramento. Personal touches, including photos, paintings and antiques from the deVere White home in Ireland, were added to complete the masterpiece. European and American sports are always on the big screens. Brothers Henry (seated) and Simon deVere (standing, third from left) are shown here along with executive chef Wes Nilssen and managing partner Josey McCarter. The food is classically Irish, including sliders, sandwiches, Granny's shepherd's pie, bangers and mash and a fry-up made with bacon brined in-house. Over two dozen Irish whiskeys are featured, including at least six types of Jameson.

1521 L Street
916.231.9947
deverespub.com

ELLA DINING ROOM & BAR

A Downtown Sacramento institution and premier dining destination, Ella Dining Room & Bar serves New American, farm-to-fork cuisine for lunch, dinner and happy hour, featuring entrées of seafood, steaks and pastas, small plates, salads, fresh oysters and traditional caviar service. Ella also features an award-winning wine list as well as seasonal and classic hand-crafted cocktails at its renowned bar. Acclaimed for food, service, design and ambiance, Ella has also earned numerous local awards and honors. Ella Dining Room & Bar is family owned and operated by Selland Family Restaurants co-founders, husband-and-wife chefs Randall Selland and Nancy Zimmer and their grown children, Josh Nelson and Tamera Baker. For 25 years, the Selland family has been committed to promoting local and sustainable growers, farmers and ranchers, and to creating fresh, honest and innovative dishes featuring the highest quality seasonal and regionally sourced ingredients at Ella and its sister restaurants, The Kitchen, Selland's Market-Café and OBO' Italian Table and Bar.

1131 K Street (at 12th Street)
916.443.3772
elladiningroomandbar.com

FIRESTONE PUBLIC HOUSE

Sports and happy hours have never looked, sounded and tasted so good in Sacramento as they do at Firestone Public House. This is a serious place for people in unserious moods—whether looking to unwind after work or catch a ballgame with friends. The beer menu is comprehensive and exhaustive, with 60 handles on tap. The televised sports options span the globe, from baseball and football to soccer and even cricket, depending on what's happening wherever, delivered on 22 flat-screen monitors with an unrivaled sound system. Two outdoor patios bring the party under the sun, moon and stars. Menus are classically American and locally inspired. They feature multicultural options as imagined by the owners, the Wong brothers—Mason, Curtis and Alan. Among the most popular dishes are delectable finger foods such as chicken wings, avocado eggrolls, banh mi sliders and pulled pork nachos. Firestone features salads, soups, epic pizzas (including one for breakfast), mouthwatering sandwiches, including Sriracha-candied bacon grilled cheese, and entrees such as beef potpie, baby back ribs and beer-battered fish and chips.

1132 16th Street
916.446.0888
firestonepublichouse.com

FRANK FAT'S

This venerable Chinese food restaurant in the heart of downtown is a true testament to the American dream. The founder of the eponymous eatery immigrated to America from China in 1919 at age 16 with no money or identification and managed to open one of the city's most iconic restaurants a mere 20 years later. Frank Fat's is now the anchor restaurant of the four establishments in the Fat's Family of Restaurants. It continues to impress with its fine dining menu and elegant interior 77 years later under the watchful eye of Fat's youngest son, Jerry (shown seated), general manager Phi Vong and executive chef Mike Lim. Traditional favorites include house-made pot stickers, Mandarin duck, Szechuan beef, honey walnut prawns that melt in your mouth and amazing assortments of chow mein, chow fun and fried rice, along with Fat's specialty dishes like wok-fried spare ribs, brandy-fried chicken, a special recipe wor won ton soup and their most decadent offering, a 16-ounce New York steak smothered in onions and oyster sauce. Leave room for dessert and treat yourself to the best banana cream pie in town. With dishes this iconic and an atmosphere this cool—check out the rosy-lit full bar—it's not hard to see why Fat's has drawn crowds for nearly a century.

806 L Street
916.442.7092
fatsrestaurants.com

INSIGHT COFFEE ROASTERS

A habitual spoonful of sugar and splash of milk—much less honey or syrup—only interferes with the relationship between the perfectly roasted coffee bean and the consumer. Such is the spirit at Insight Coffee Roasters, where quality coffee needs no embellishment. Established in 2011, Insight thrives on a coffee-as-lifestyle motif. Tastings, seminars and classes are offered to help customers better appreciate the journey made by Insight's internationally sourced beans from farm to roaster to brewer to cup. The attitude at Insight is perpetually friendly, relaxed and laid back. The flagship roaster and café at Southside Park anchors a growing coffee empire. Outposts can be found across from the Capitol on 10th Street, on the edge of Midtown on 16th Street at Fremont Park and in the Pavilions Shopping Center. More sites are coming, and the educational work will never cease.

1901 8th Street
1014 10th Street
1615 16th Street
916.905.7904
insightcoffee.com

MA JONG'S ASIAN DINER

Never mind the ancient game played with plastic tiles. At this downtown restaurant, the name Ma Jong pays tribute to the matriarchs of a centuries-old family dynasty and combines the culinary cultures of Japan, Thailand, Vietnam and China. The unique flavors from those countries reveal their profiles in each of Ma Jong's dishes. Aromas mingle and create an atmosphere at once homey and exotic. Daily specials feature meats, fresh fish and crisp vegetables, simmering in soy, teriyaki, basil and peanut sauces. The interior of Ma Jong's Asian Diner is meant to evoke images of a village, with natural wood countertops, low-back seats and several communal tables. Dangling lanterns cast a soft glow on the exposed ductwork and brick walls to remind customers they are in the heart of the city enjoying adventurous Asian fare. Watching over the experience is a 300-year-old Buddha. Downtown workers bundle off takeaway boxes of Shanghai spicy chow mein. Central city residents call orders in and await the arrival of the delivery rickshaw emblazoned with Ma Jong's enigmatic face. The restaurant is a convenient stop for theatergoers eager for a quick bite before curtain time at the Community Center Theater one block east.

1431 L Street
916.442.7555
majongs.com

SOUTH

On a quiet stretch of 11th Street in the Southside Park neighborhood, a little bistro combines two modern trends in neighborhood dining: unaffected casualness and back-to-basics cooking. The owners are N'Gina and Ian Kavookjian, and they base their menu and restaurant's philosophy on timeless traditions of Southern cooking. Or, as the owners describe it, "At South, we are not trying to reinvent the wheel, we are just trying to express 200 years of our family's story on a 12-inch plate." The family history is a gorgeous mix of traditional Southern and Cajun cooking styles. Yams, fried green tomatoes and hushpuppies are all on point. The standout dish is the fried chicken, a classic take on a familiar meal that becomes something remarkable at South. People talk of South's fried chicken in hushed voices and reverent tones, and many knowing fans believe there is no better example of this Southern kitchen essential, at least not west of the Mississippi. Order at the counter and then select your table inside or on the charming patio for service.

2005 11th Street
916.382.9722
weheartfriedchicken.com

PUBLIC ART

Framed by two rivers with the Sierra Nevada and Coast Ranges rising on its horizons, Sacramento is blessed with natural beauty. Today, the creative arts are supplementing the community's natural treasures, and Sacramento is increasingly recognized for public artworks that surprise, inspire and delight. Dozens of public art installations can be found while strolling in neighborhoods across the city's grid. Monumental and intimate works can be discovered along streets, in buildings and parks throughout the community. These artworks celebrate the culture of the city and contribute to Sacramento's uniqueness. The works are possible because Sacramento is home to a "percent for art" program that reserves a portion of construction dollars from civic development projects for public art. The result is the "Art in Public Places" program, administered by the Sacramento Metropolitan Arts Commission. The program is committed to expanding the public's knowledge and experience of the visual arts. Maps are available with directions to most of the major permanent artworks on display downtown. Multiple blocks are described, but tours can be broken into easily manageable mini-treks of artistic discovery.

916.808.3992
sacmetroarts.org

HOT ITALIAN

Their mission was to build a place where delicious pizza brings people together. Their motto became *tutto e possibile*—anything is possible. The formula worked. Anything is possible at Hot Italian. Consider the Bortolami, a celebration of house-made fennel sausage, seasonal mushrooms, tomato sauce, smoked mozzarella and treviso radicchio. Or the Fiori, which combines prosciutto parma, mozzarella, mushrooms, tomato sauce, arugula and Bariani truffle oil. Beyond its remarkably inventive pizza, Hot Italian celebrates a joy for life. The restaurant is filled with friends eager to celebrate spontaneity in art, music, design and sports. The owners are Andrea Lepore, an Italian-American from a family of artists, and Fabrizio Cercatore, an artistic *pizzaiolo*, or master pizza maker, from the Italian Riviera region of Cinque Terre. They built a European-style community gathering place, where soccer matches and cycling events play on monitors and Vespa scooters supplement the space. Gelato in flavors like caramel salato, chocolate orange, limon, peanut butter chip, stracciatella and white mint chip complete the magic.

1627 16th Street
916.444.3000
hotitalian.net

PRESERVATION & CO.

In the hands of Jason Poole (shown) and Brad Peters, pickled habanero pepper chips become a work of gastronomical art. Poole and Peters are business partners and brining experts who preserve delicious and healthy produce from local farms without artificial colors, flavors or preservatives. They capture zesty flavors that make tongues dance. The team behind the "Sacramento born and brined" brand specializes in hand-packed products created in their compact location behind a roll-up door along an industrial stretch of 19th Street. From this hideaway, they sell to more than 400 retail locations across the country. Preservation & Co. features an inventory that includes cocktail mixes—Bloody Mary mix, blackberry and jalapeño margarita—and pickles, sriracha sauces, citrus rosemary salt and ghost pepper salt, plus bar and pantry supplies and clothing. The pickles alone are amazing, from balsamic beet slices, habanero chips, jalapeño onion strips and cayenne carrot sticks, to hefeweizen bread and butter chips, hickory Brussels sprouts, horseradish green beans and black pepper asparagus. The Midtown outpost of Preservation & Co. is a gathering place for flavor aficionados, who appreciate the shop's liberal sampling policy.

1717 19th Street, Suite B
916.706.1044
preservationandco.com

TIME TESTED BOOKS

Behind a brick façade on 21st Street, inside a 19th-century building, Time Tested Books is a portal to another time and place. Since 1981, owner Peter Keat has made it his mission to stock his cozy bookshop with an impressive array of new and used titles, including rare and out-of-print books and vinyl records. Keat and his knowledgeable staff assist guests in search of specific and difficult-to-find titles. And for clients hoping to reduce their own collections, Time Tested Books buys and trades books and records. The shop serves as host to a variety of events such as author signings, readings, lectures and musical performances, all certain to inspire and enlighten the book lover and culture devotee in all of us. Be sure to say hello to Keat's adorable dog, Marco, when making a visit.

1114 21st Street
916.447.5696
timetestedbooks.blogspot.com

INSIDE *Old Sac*

Old Sacramento is a national historic landmark district dating from the mid–19th century. The raised wooden sidewalks were built to handle floodwater from the Sacramento River.

Most of the historic Victorian-era buildings have been authentically restored and now house restaurants, shops and museums. Look for decorative design touches from the time of Spanish rule in California.

The landmark Tower Bridge glows golden across the Sacramento River to West Sacramento. The Sacramento River Train runs fun excursions from the historic depot.

Many festivals and events take place in Old Sacramento. The district also contains memorials to the founders of the city, the state and the Transcontinental Railroad, including the Theodore Judah monument and the Pony Express statue.

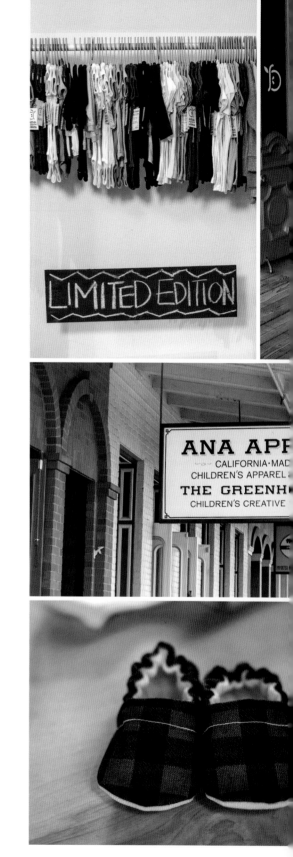

ANA APPLE

An enchanted dream world for the younger set comes to life at Ana Apple. Owner Ana Manzano imagined a shop where parents could find unique, handmade clothing for their little ones, plus activity space for classes and special events that "cultivate creative curiosity" among children and young adults. It's all pulled together in a stunning historic Old Sacramento storefront. Manzano, a former freelance photographer, gained momentum for her shop by winning the 2014 Calling All Dreamers competition sponsored by the Downtown Sacramento Partnership. Manzano is a skilled seamstress who first created kids' clothes for family and friends in her living room. New editions of those designs, plus other California-made products, are displayed on apple boxes and carts.

114 K Street
916.737.5272
anaapple.com

The GREEN HOUSE

CREATIVITY COMES IN ALL FORMS.
(AND SOMETIMES IT'S MESSY.)
WE BELIEVE CREATIVE EXPRESSION
HELPS CHILDREN BUILD CONFIDENCE,
DEVELOP A UNIQUE VOICE,
THINK CRITICALLY AND APPROACH
THE WORLD WITH MORE COMPASSION,
TO PUT IT SIMPLY
WE STRIVE TO HELP OUR STUDENTS
LEAVE A LITTLE MORE INSPIRED
THAN THEY

RIO CITY CAFÉ

Husband-and-wife owners Mark and Stephanie Miller opened Rio City Café in 1994 in a stylishly rustic building designed to resemble a steamship warehouse from the late 1800s. The concept was perfect. The restaurant blends seamlessly with the quaint, historic charms of the Old Sacramento riverfront. The casual setting, overseen by general manager Scott Meier, features indoor and outdoor seating, room for banquets and Tower Bridge and riverfront views that match the inspiration of a fresh, farm-to-fork menu. While Rio City dishes are distinctively Californian, executive chef Scott Swanson (shown seated) combines international ingredients—favorites include coconut prawns, the zesty tostada bowl and the steak brochette— to please diverse palates. Specialty cocktails are Rio City trademarks. The wine list features popular selections from Napa and other California labels.

1110 Front Street
916.442.8226
riocitycafe.com

THE FIREHOUSE RESTAURANT

Smoked tenderloin carpaccio. Lobster bisque. Filet mignon. Veal porterhouse. Famed for perennial excellence, The Firehouse Restaurant has been a not-to-be-missed destination for more than 55 years. Housed in a building from 1853 that served as home for the Sacramento No. 3 Fire Brigade, the elegant dining spot was one of Ronald Reagan's favorite places in Sacramento during his eight years as governor—and it's easy to see why. In addition to its rich history, evidenced by it stunning façade and low-lit, grand interior, The Firehouse offers a menu of gourmet classics, matched by a legendary wine list with more than 2,100 labels. Visit the wine cellar to view more than 16,000 bottles housed in the cool depths. Let General Manager, Wine Director and Sommelier Mario Ortiz—a Firehouse fixture for more than 40 years—introduce the Vault, a magnificent collection of very rare Californian and European wines. It's no wonder The Firehouse has played host to a star-studded guest list over the years, including Clint Eastwood, Muhammad Ali, Andy Warhol, George Foreman, Michael Jordan and every California governor since the last one to become president.

1112 2nd Street
916.442.4772
firehouseoldsac.com

ARTISTS' COLLABORATIVE GALLERY

As the oldest artistic cooperative in Sacramento, the Artists' Collaborative Gallery is precisely what the title suggests: a gathering place for nearly 40 local artists to display and sell beautiful wares. Fine art and ceramics, glass, gourds, jewelry, metal, photography, textiles, wire sculpture, wood and fiber art are available. The member artists, who are invited into the collective studio and store by the collegial membership, are award-winning creators. They come from a wide variety of backgrounds. Inspiring artwork stands out against the dark wood floors and white walls of the converted historical Old Sacramento storefront. Visitors gain a sense of having stepped into a wonderful world of whimsy and creativity. Guests are certain to meet at least one of the artists whose work is on display—the creative talents take turns working in the store. They greet guests and answer questions about the artwork and make the experience truly collaborative.

129 K Street
916.444.7125
artcollab.com

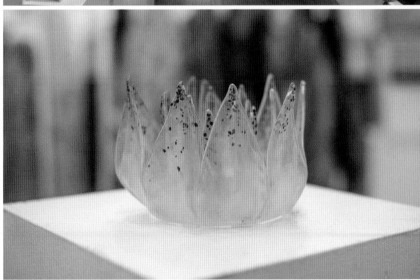

TEN22

Three essentials of hospitality—eat, drink, relax—comprise the mission at this comfortable Old Sacramento hangout created by the owners of the upmarket Firehouse Restaurant down the street. Ten22 features a lovely patio and cozy interior booths where guests unwind over a diverse menu. Drinks range from local craft beers—there are 24 handles—to craft cocktails and a comprehensive wine list with more than 110 selections. Executive Chef Jay Veregge has created a New American menu for lunch and dinner, highlighted by ingredients culled from regional farmers and transformed into mouthwatering dishes. Examples include butternut squash and onion crostini, a Portobello mushroom sandwich served with wilted escarole and tomato jam on ciabatta, and Wood Stone pizzas that incorporate deliciously unique combinations—including cauliflower and gorgonzola, prosciutto and leeks and butternut squash and sausage. Sides such as truffle pommes frites, grown-up mac & cheese and polenta fries—plus desserts like tiramisu bread pudding and fair-trade-chocolate layer cake—complete the experience. All of the above make eating, drinking and relaxing simple pleasures at Ten22.

1022 2nd Street
916.441.2211
ten22oldsac.com

HISTORIC R&: CORRIDOR

FISHFACE
POKE BAR

INSIDE R Street

Once a thriving warehouse district, the R Street Corridor is being transformed into a vibrant city neighborhood with locally owned cafés, shops, services and entertainment venues. Sometimes called the Creative Corridor, its vintage industrial buildings now provide a gritty, open canvas for some of Sacramento's many artists, artisans and entrepreneurs.

Located in the heart of the R Street Corridor, WAL (Warehouse Artist Lofts) is a mixed-income community with four stories of apartments above ground-floor shops and restaurants. It's a place where creative individuals and households can live, work, learn and collaborate with one another.

BENJAMINS SHOES

Clearly a man devoted to well-tailored classics, Benjamin Schwartz discovered an old textbook on shoemaking about six years ago and dived headlong into the bespoke shoe crafting business. Today, he runs his unique shop at the back of the Public Market in the bottom floor of the Warehouse Artist Lofts. Benjamins Shoes is the only handmade artisanal shoe shop in Sacramento. The store features a product line that combines the casual look of a boat shoe with the upscale aesthetic of a man's dress slipper. Each item is handmade by Schwartz in a range of fabrics, including high-quality leather and luxurious Loro Piana cashmere from Italy. The shoes feature leather laces, water-resistant rubber soles and canvas toeboxes for structure and durability. Benjamins Shoes provides the ideal finish to an outfit that needs a precise measure of individuality. Every pair is made in an extremely limited run to ensure the bespoke aura.

1104 R Street, Suite 130
benjamins-shoes.com

CAFÉ BERNARDO

Seasonal menus with fresh, locally sourced ingredients and creative bar concepts unique to each Café Bernardo location make these eateries neighborhood favorites from Midtown to the R Street Corridor to Downtown. A cornerstone of Sacramento's legendary Paragary Restaurant Group, Café Bernardo combines an informal, European-style café environment with the quality and attention to detail that have been Randy and Stacy Paragary's standard for decades. Certain favorites endure year round, such as the mushroom, Jarlsberg cheese and parsley salad and Thai noodle salad, which brims with chicken, carrots, cucumbers, scallions and thin noodles in spicy peanut dressing. Sandwiches are globally inspired and include banh mi, Cubano and mushroom melt. The burgers and pizzettas rate among the best in town. Lines form for weekend breakfast, where fans savor the Bernardo Breakfast Sandwich (two farm eggs, bacon, Romesco, grilled onion and white cheddar with herbed potatoes), amaretto brioche French toast and whole-grain blueberry pancakes.

1431 R Street
916.930.9191

2726 Capitol Avenue
916.443.1180

1000 K Street
916.446.9800
paragarys.com

ROXIE DELI

When Chris and Amy Tannous purchased Priceless Market in East Sacramento in 2004, they bought a piece of history. The market at the corner of C and 33rd Streets was a neighborhood institution, and the new owners were eager to build upon the reputation. Like the market, Roxie Deli has deep roots—Chris's parents opened a Roxie Deli in San Francisco in the mid-1970s. Chris was 6 years old when the San Francisco shop began. He stood on a milk crate to reach the counter. The youthful tradition continues with the Tannouses' own children at the East Sac eatery. Roxie Deli expanded in 2009 and added smoked meats. Loyal customers at the original location and new R Street store line up for tri-tip, ribs and specials. Menus include breakfast, lunch and dinner and renowned Roxie sandwiches, plus catering, hand-selected microbrews and craft sodas.

1800 15th Street
916.447.6943

3340 C Street
916.443.5402
roxiedeli.com

FISH FACE POKE BAR

Hawaiian chefs invented poke as a fresh fish appetizer. Sacramento chef Billy Ngo, whose Kru sushi restaurant took Japanese raw fish delicacies to a new stratosphere, is letting his imagination roam across the deep blue Pacific with Fish Face Poke Bar. Under Ngo's guidance, humble Hawaiian poke breaks free from its appetizer limitations and becomes a complete meal, complex, surprising and satisfying. Every dish of Fresh Face Poke is made to order with green and white onions, seaweed, sesame seeds and a choice of proteins—ahi tuna, octopus, shrimp, Ora King Salmon, Passmore Ranch sturgeon, mussels and tofu. The sauces—sesame soy, spicy kimchi ponzu, wasabi soy, creamy cilantro pesto or yuzu ponzu—make poke unique and imaginative. Fish Face Poke Bar gets the customers into the game by providing ingredients to customize the dish, including cilantro, jalapeño, rice crisps, crunchy garlic, daikon sprouts, macadamia nuts, seasonal fruit, fish roe and seaweed. The bar is stocked with local beers and stellar sake.

1104 R Street, Suite 100
916.706.0605
fishfacepokebar.com

IRON HORSE TAVERN

One hundred sixty years ago, passenger trains rumbled down R Street from Sacramento to Folsom. Next came freight trains serving endless warehouses. Today, locomotive history merges with industrial cool and the sleek modernity of a revitalized neighborhood at Iron Horse Tavern. The newest dining destination from the Wong family restaurateurs Mason, Curtis and Alan, Iron Horse features a style that combines industrial and international design. Vintage touches including reclaimed wood and hexagonal tile floors share space. The bar is beautiful, with black anodized steel and a pounded copper top. Blown-glass lighting fixtures, leather banquettes and a model locomotive perched beneath the antique tin ceiling make the atmosphere simultaneously edgy and comfortable. The vibe continues with the gastropub menu overseen by Chef Christian Palmos. Iron Horse offers breakfast and brunch, with pancakes, frittatas and eggs, plus salads, sandwiches, pizzas and small plates made with locally sourced produce and a popular macaroni and cheese bar for lunch and dinner. Signature cocktails, beer and wine are available on the patio, which opens to R Street and the city's hippest old and new neighborhood.

1800 15th Street
916.448.4488
ironhorsetavern.net

MAGPIE CAFÉ

From its first meal in 2009, Magpie Café has defined the term "farm-to-fork." Seasonal menus, locally sourced ingredients and a sustainable environment have been goals consistently met by this ambitious restaurant, which expanded from its R Street home uptown to 16th Street in 2014. Co-owners Ed Roehr and Janel Inouye maintain the original location as a base for their powerhouse catering business (which provided their introduction to the hospitality industry). The new building fits ideally with the Magpie mentality. Called 16 Powerhouse, the space features LEED-certified solar water heating and other green energy features, and Roehr and Inouye link menu items directly to the seasons. Favorites include crispy pork belly, a trio of dragon mushrooms, Pacific Northwest crab and shrimp Louie, a cheese plate sourced from Marin and a Kingbird Farm special for breakfast. Wine, beer and spirits from the Sacramento region and the Bay Area are featured.

1601 16th Street
916.452.7594
magpiecafe.com

NIDO BAKERY CAFÉ BY MAGPIE

Maple pecan scone. Carrot pecan coconut muffin. Brownie with hazelnut. Black bottom cupcake. Thyme ice cream sandwich. Such sugary concoctions become masterpieces at Nido Bakery Café. The café occupies the original R Street location of Magpie Café and is owned by the creative couple behind Magpie, Ed Roehr and Janel Inouye. But Nido differs from its full-service cousin by focusing on sweet treats and a tidy menu of intriguing, locally sourced dishes such as spicy chicken wings, heirloom bean chili, a sausage sandwich on a pretzel bun served with kale salad, plus pizza and sandwiches. The café is cozy, and the cooking emphasis is made apparent by the size of the kitchen—it occupies two-thirds of the space. Intriguing selections of wine and beer are available to pair with a simple meal and delicious dessert.

1409 R Street
916.668.7594
hellonido.com

SHOKI RAMEN HOUSE

Under the guidance of chef and owner Yasushi Ueyama, ramen becomes a culinary art form that is as much about health and well-being as flavor. Following a successful career as a restaurateur and chef in Kobe, Japan, Ueyama and his family arrived in the U.S. in 2001 and opened restaurants in Folsom before he founded Shoki Ramen House with co-owner and wife, Kathy, on R Street. They recently opened a second location on 21st Street in Land Park. Ueyama trained at university as a nutritionist and wanted to bring the Japanese fine dining style, known as *kaiseki*, to Sacramento. When *kaiseki* traditions proved a challenge for local diners, Ueyama shifted to the made-from-scratch, wholesome deliciousness of traditional ramen. Shoki Ramen House broths and dishes include no preservatives or MSG. Ueyama purchases ingredients from local organic farms and uses cage-free, organic eggs and grass-fed beef in his two famous ramen varieties, blended (featuring wafu broth, a Japanese traditional soup) and vegetable, served at a precise temperature to maintain the soup's immense nutrient value.

1201 R Street
2530 21st Street
916.441.0011
shokiramenhouse.com

INSIDE *Midtown*

From the Sutter District to Boulevard Park and Poverty Ridge, Midtown not only offers an intriguing mix of boutiques, bars, galleries and restaurants, but also a collection of smaller neighborhoods.

Historic homes and tree-lined streets invite comfortable strolling and cycling. The mix and density of residential and commercial properties are unique to Sacramento.

Sutter's Fort captures pioneer life at the dawn of the California Gold Rush. John Sutter built the fort as the base of his agricultural empire.

This neighborhood hosts a popular year-round Saturday farmers market, creating a vibrant community gathering place. The Second Saturday Art Walk attracts throngs of folks excited by art and creativity.

CENTRO COCINA MEXICANA

Regional Mexican cooking inspired by recipes, ingredients and styles rarely found in Sacramento have made Centro Cocina Mexicana a festive Midtown jewel for more than two decades. Paragary Restaurant Group Executive Chef Kurt Spataro, whose attention to detail and insistence on authenticity have established his legacy as one of Sacramento's most respected chefs, spent months observing kitchens in Mexico's coastal towns and inland cities to prepare the original Centro Cocina Mexicana menu. Repeat journeys have brought new menu items, all faithful to their original geography. Centro's renditions of ceviche de pescado and empanadas, along with tacos, burritos, grilled meats and shrimp and mole, have created a generation of devotees. Centro's colorful atmosphere boasts a constellation of metal star lanterns dangling from the exposed wooden ceiling, decorative crosses and vessels, a vintage motorcycle floating above a window and touches of pink and blue on the walls. The full-service bar features more than 300 brands of tequila, cold Mexican draft beer and everything in between.

2730 J Street
916.442.2552
paragarys.com

FLEET FEET SPORTS/BOUTIQUE

Runners across Northern California regard Fleet Feet Sports and Fleet Feet Boutique as a presence far beyond a typical retail sports store. With a deep inventory and personal, expert advice from staffers who share a runner's passion, Fleet Feet is more pro shop than store. Owners Jan and Pat Sweeney say their goal is to "bring our town to its feet," and they mean it. Fleet Feet Sports was founded in Sacramento in 1976 and grew into a nationally franchised operation. Eighteen years ago, the Sweeney team bought the original Sacramento store. They added the Fleet Feet Boutique next door 11 years later. Time passes and trends change. But the original spirit remains the hallmark of the Fleet Feet shopping experience on J Street. Fleet Feet Sports focuses on shoes and clothing for running and active lifestyles. The Boutique offers women urban-casual and comfortable fashions for work, weekends and travel. Completing the Fleet Feet experience is a team of 40 employees, including training divisions that each year help more than 2,500 athletes gain their footing.

2311 & 2315 J Street
916.442.3338
fleetfeetsacramento.com

PARAGARY'S

A bustling bistro blossomed to life on the edge of Midtown in the summer of 2015, delivered by Sacramento's leading restaurateur in a space he knows intimately well. Randy Paragary, wife Stacy and Executive Chef Kurt Spataro spent more than a year remodeling the corner of 28th and N Streets for the third time since 1975. Four decades ago, the restaurant was a fern bar called Lord Beaverbrook's. A remodel in 1983 brought the namesake Paragary's to 28th Street, which gave way to the current chic new environment of a French-inspired bistro, with intricate black and white encaustic concrete tile floors, simple tables and sleek banquettes that manage to be both quaint and contemporarily cool. The light and airy interiors open to Paragary's renowned patio with waterfalls, 60-year-old olive trees and a fireplace. Spataro brings his precise touch to a menu that delivers California twists on French classics. The croque monsieur sandwich served on toasted brioche with gruyere and Niman Ranch ham is completed by an inspired béchamel sauce. Mary's chicken liver mousse comes with an onion confit and marsala sauce. The wood oven–roasted mussels served with lemon, olive oil, shallots, garlic, herbs and grilled bread are delicious. Forty years and counting, Paragary's thrives.

1401 28th Street
916.457.5737
paragarys.com

SACRAMENTO NATURAL FOODS CO-OP

Every lifestyle—omnivore, vegan, raw, paleo, organic, gluten-free and carnivore—can find sustenance at the Sacramento Natural Foods Co-op. The "Co-op," as fans call the store, was founded as a natural food collective in 1972, a time when organic and natural foods were rare in Sacramento. Today, thousands of members maintain ownership in the co-op, but you don't have to be an owner to enjoy the bountiful selections found along every aisle. The produce department is 100 percent organic. Many items, including honey, olive oil, jams, cheese, wine and beer, are purchased from local producers. Each produce item is marked with the farm name and location where the food was grown. Educational programs encourage the community to cook, eat and live well. There are cooking classes for all ages, wellness workshops led by local health professionals and farm tours. Artisan products are available daily, and the deli has devoted fans lined up at lunchtime. For warehouse shoppers, the co-op carries more than 700 items to purchase in bulk.

2820 R Street
916.455.2667
sacfoodcoop.com

SUZIE BURGER

A 1950s burger joint comes alive within a former "Orbit" style gas station at the corner of 29th and P Streets, complete with a pointed roof that looks like it migrated from Mars, circa 1960. Suzie Burger makes the mash-up of eras work like magic in a setting that can never be duplicated, with outstanding, proudly American food to seal the deal. Vintage architecture and clever interior design make Suzie Burger worth the first visit, but return trips will be driven by the namesake burgers, cheesesteaks and other mid-century delights produced by inventive brothers Matt and Fred Haines. Matt is the numbers guy, Fred the chef. The partnership flourishes thanks to high-quality food, starting with 100 percent USDA Choice beef, along with hand-cut fries, the classic Philly cheesesteak, foot-long hot dogs and Suzie's famous Chocolate Brick Sundae. Not exactly what the doctor ordered, but delicious every time.

2820 P Street
916.455.3500
suzieburger.com

SUN & SOIL JUICE COMPANY

Molly Brown (shown at left in photo) and Tatiana Kaiser opened Sun & Soil in June 2014 with a simple mission: infuse raw, organic nutrition into the community through delicious juice, smoothies and food with produce from local farms. Sun & Soil seeks out the freshest, non-GMO fruits and vegetables to ensure that all drinks are naturally raw, vegan and gluten-free with no processed sugars. Committed to protecting the environment from the inside out, Brown and Kaiser reduce their carbon footprint with a glass bottle exchange program as they move from plastic or Styrofoam options. Sun & Soil specializes in cold-pressed juice, which minimizes heat and the oxidation of nutrients. The process places two tons of pressure onto the pulp to extract the juices. It releases three to five times the amount of micronutrients, enzymes and flavor compared to traditional juicing methods. The cold-press method allows for a shelf life of up to five days, making it easy for customers to enjoy fresh juice as a part of their daily nutrition. Sun & Soil offers an array of flavors and guidance to help reboot digestive systems in most delicious ways. Also featured are organic snacks such as goji bites and house-made granola, served within a quaint, sunshine-yellow storefront.

1912 P Street
916.341.0327
sunandsoiljuice.com

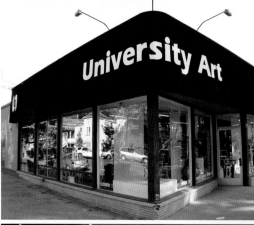

UNIVERSITY ART

Creativity finds no boundaries at University Art, where plush puppets, notebooks and magnets share shelf space with paintbrushes, pens, charcoal pencils, paper, ink, frames, canvas and paints for every palette. Founded in 1948 by two sisters determined to provide a reasonably priced one-stop shop for artists, sculptors and writers, University Art succeeds far beyond those post-war expectations. Today, University Art honors its founding mission but has expanded to include services as diverse as Sacramento's creative community. The shop offers custom framing and art education materials, along with an array of No. 2 pencils, journals and calendars. Manager David Saalsaa has even turned University Art into a gallery: rotating installations brighten the front window. More than 100 artists have enjoyed showings at University Art, the art store with everything.

2601 J Street
916.443.5721
universityart.com

THE WATERBOY

Classic European delicacies such as steak tartare, sautéed veal sweetbreads, braised lamb shank and simmering bouillabaisse blend with locally sourced ingredients to make The Waterboy a treasured destination on Sacramento's culinary map. Established in 1996 by homegrown chef and owner Rick Mahan, The Waterboy builds upon the region's farm-to-fork legacy. Mahan gathers the freshest produce, fish and meats to create masterful dishes worthy of a French countryside bistro or a northern Italian ristorante. The chef, whose professional career began at age 16, pairs delicious ingredients and highly polished skills with a diverse wine list and full bar featuring artisanal cocktails and aperitifs. Desserts are made fresh daily. The Waterboy was inspired by a journey Mahan took to France. The chef consistently delivers on his goal to create intriguing European-style fare with California ingredients, no passport needed.

2000 Capitol Avenue
916.498.9891
waterboyrestaurant.com

BIBA RISTORANTE ITALIANO

Legendary chef, cookbook author and restaurant owner Biba Caggiano has bustled nonstop between kitchen and dining area, greeting guests and checking pasta dishes at the elegant restaurant for 30 years. Caggiano and husband, Vince, a physician renowned for his work in oncology, have made this special place a component of their home and life. For a generation, Biba has set the standard for professional service—including nightly live piano thanks to musicians Rich O'Day (shown), Claudette Stone and Reggie Graham—the best seasonal ingredients and exquisite preparation and presentation. These days, Vince oversees the wine list while Biba directs the kitchen and front of the house, somehow simultaneously. Born in Bologna, Italy, Biba arrived in Sacramento with her husband in 1969. She entertained friends at home with recipes liberated from her mother's kitchen. She was persuaded to stage informal cooking classes, which expanded to television segments and cookbooks—nine volumes are currently in print. Biba Ristorante and the creative force behind it are both Sacramento treasures.

2801 Capitol Avenue
916.455.2422
biba-restaurant.com

FEDERALIST PUBLIC HOUSE

Marvin (shown) and Bridgette Maldonado are in pursuit of the perfect pizza. The Florin High School sweethearts and owners of Federalist Public House—the infinitely cool farm-to-fork restaurant in the alley between Capitol Avenue and N, 20th and 21st Streets—spent a year researching pizza before opening their eatery in December 2014. The couple's three sons served as taste testers. The menu features a variety of signature wood-fired pizzas under the direction of Chef Shannon McElroy, plus a rotating selection of local craft beers, wine, nitro coffee and kombucha served at communal tables that run alongside a bocce court. The restaurant and pub are housed in giant steel shipping containers—a design-driven idea from Marvin—in the converted backyard of a Victorian house built in the Federalist style, which inspired the restaurant's name.

2009 Matsui Alley
916.661.6134
federalistpublichouse.com

THAI BASIL

Determined to maintain the authenticity of home-cooked meals from Thailand, Prayoon Sununsangthong opened the first Thai Basil in Roseville in 1995. She brought the flavors of her pantry to the region. Now her three daughters—Wanni, Kannika and Suleka Sun-Lindley, who runs the J Street location—each own and operate Thai Basil restaurants as a tribute to the cuisine of their mother. Menu items at the Midtown location include traditional dishes such as pad-kee-mow (or "drunken noodles," thick rice noodles pan-fried in spicy soy sauce with chopped garlic, chilies, tomatoes and Thai basil), red, yellow and green curries, spicy eggplant, pineapple fried rice, tom kha gai soup (creamy coconut milk broth infused with lemon grass, kaffir lime leaves, onions, cilantro, mushrooms, a touch of lime juice and roasted curry), plus appetizers that include spring rolls, tofu satay and fried prawns. Upstairs, VEG presents vegetarian and vegan options, with food made according to the principles of Ayurveda—the art of living in harmony with nature. Vegetarian specialties are offered for brunch, lunch, happy hour and dinner. Coffee, tea and libations bring balance to body and palate.

2431 J Street
916.442.7690
thaibasilrestaurant.com

LUMENS LIGHT & LIVING

A dazzling collection of ceiling lights, indoor and outdoor wall sconces, table lamps, floor lamps, architectural lighting and all objects illuminative captivate and inspire across a 4,000-square-foot showroom at Lumens Light & Living. Styles are as varied as the hardware, with Arts & Crafts, contemporary, mid-century modern and modern represented among the thousands of lighting options. In a commitment to support independent and emerging artists, founders Ken Plumlee (shown at left) and Peter Weight created space within their showroom for artisan lighting alongside designs from brands such as Alessi, Kartell and Philippe Starck. The Lumens team of lighting experts can help with technical specifications and design plans to bring a homeowner's ideas to completion. And the best designs in modern home and personal accessory products are featured in their Design Shop within the store. Also worthy of a visit is Lumens Annex at 712 R Street, where clearance and open-box items are offered.

2028 K Street
916.444.5585
lumens.com

THE RED RABBIT KITCHEN & BAR

Owners Matt Nurge and John Bays—who serve as barman and chef, respectively—focus on all things local at The Red Rabbit. They present food served with boundless sophistication and local ingredients and run an endlessly bespoke operation, making as much as possible by hand. Appropriately, even the syrups for The Red Rabbit's eclectic cocktails are created in-house. The juices are fresh-squeezed and the herbs are hand-muddled. Even the wines are a celebration of California's hands-on viticulture. With a space that manages to be cool, industrial, warm and welcoming at once, The Red Rabbit provides comfort from the moment a customer arrives. The lighting is low, the wood mellow and dark, and the brick walls are well aged. The menu is an eclectic mix of classics with a twist— pork belly kimchi tacos, fried Brussels sprouts and bacon, beet carpaccio, rabbit Bolognese, vegan mushroom potato curry. Brunch and happy hour presentations are exceedingly popular.

2718 J Street
916.706.2275
theredrabbit.net

SKOOL

Inspired by its big brother in San Francisco, Skool on K brings an inventive, nuanced and sophisticated taste of Japanese-influenced seafood dishes to Sacramento. The restaurant is directed by two experienced husband-and-wife teams. Owners and operators are Andy Mirabell and Olia Kedik. Executive chef is Toshihiro Nagano, with his wife Hiroko Nagano handling duties as pastry chef and creative director. The creative side of Skool is apparent from first glance, and the front of the house and kitchen have run with precision since the restaurant opened in early 2016. Skool represents a new direction for Midtown, with the space playing on cozy minimalism, black-and-white wall art, a grid setup of simple wooden tables and chairs and a smattering of Japanese kitchen regalia. The name *Skool* becomes not merely a play on the definition of a group of fish, but an inspiration for classroom design elements. Menus feature small bites, as well as cured and raw dishes. Specialties include ocean trout, sardine and king salmon tartare, all served with casual grace. Menus are printed on lined notebook paper and secured to boards with No. 2 pencils.

2319 K Street
916.737.5767
skoolonkstreet.com

MIDTOWN FARMERS MARKET

Each Saturday morning from 8 A.M. to 1 P.M., the Midtown Farmers Market transforms the outdoor community center of the historic and eclectic Midtown neighborhood. Dozens of vendors with fresh, locally grown and frequently organic produce and flowers blend with numerous artisanal food sellers. Shoppers wander and sample regionally grown honey, fresh almond milk, zesty beef jerky and hand-rolled pastas. A mini food truck prepares Belgian waffles. Barbequed meats are grilled and smoked to fall off the bone as local residents and visitors enjoy their meals at nearby picnic tables. Kombucha and juices made fresh in the neighborhood are available as finishing touches. Children play in a dedicated area called the Budding Foodies zone. Musical artists perform while crowds gather, make purchases and linger in the relaxed, informal fellowship the Midtown Farmers Market brings to the neighborhood.

20th and J Streets
exploremidtown.org

TAPA THE WORLD

Traditional Spanish and Basque tapas, live music and inspired cocktails are a tradition at Tapa the World, founded in 1994 by siblings Conni Levis and Paul Ringstrom. Conni is shown here with executive chef Marcos Murillo (center) and bar manager Chris Callaway (right). This lively restaurant offers a sophisticated assortment of small-plate dishes to be shared and savored. Tapa the World is popular for *la comida* (lunch) and *la cena* (dinner) and all the *bebidas* (drinks) and *postres* (desserts) in between. A typical Tapa the World adventure begins with tortilla Española (the "Spanish poor man's" potato cake cooked in olive oil with onion and egg), followed by jamon Serrano (dry cured and aged Spanish ham) and champiñones al ajillo (mushrooms sautéed in olive oil, garlic, parsley and white wine). From there, aceitunas (a selection of olives from Spain and around the world) serves as an interlude, with patatas bravas (fried potato cubes with spicy tomato sauce), calamares fritos (calamari dusted with Spanish pimentón and lightly fried with Romesco sauce), and berenjenas (eggplant, breaded and fried, topped with a cool tomato, garlic and herb compote and shredded Parmesan) to follow, all at a relaxing pace. The house-made sangria is direct from Iberia.

2115 J Street
916.442.4353
tapatheworld.com

REVOLUTION WINES

As the city's only fully operational urban winery, Revolution Wines is devoted to the idea that locally produced wine and food is the best expression of the Sacramento landscape, or terroir. Revolution is owned by Gina Genshlea (shown) and her husband, Joe. From its headquarters on S Street, Revolution excels as a full-service operation, combining the winery, tasting room and eatery in one location. Using fruit from Yolo Vineyards, Aparicio Vineyards, Gandyhill Vineyards and Sutter Ranch Vineyards, Revolution's family-owned and -operated facility crushes, ferments and bottles in the city's midst. The sophisticated kitchen offers Italian classics such as fritto misto, an antipasto plate and a steak panzanella salad. Heartier fare is also available, such as steak frites and Prince Edward Island mussels, to complement exclusive wine pairings for oenophiles and foodies alike.

2831 S Street
916.444.7711
rev.wine

TRUE

"Fashion for Good" is the motive and motto behind TRUE boutique in Midtown. TRUE stands for Totally Recycled Urban Exchange. The concept for the 2,350-square-foot retail clothing boutique was established in 2015 by WEAVE, Women Escaping a Violent Environment, the non-profit organization that serves as the primary provider of crisis intervention services for survivors of domestic violence and sexual assault in Sacramento County. One hundred percent of proceeds earned through the buying, selling and trading of fashion items at TRUE fund programs and services to empower survivors of domestic violence and sexual assault. The goal is for WEAVE clients to regain independence and live their lives free of violence. The shop features clothing, shoes and accessories. TRUE customers contribute to making the community a better and safer place for hundreds of local women, men and children.

1900 K Street
trueclothing.org

TEMPLE COFFEE ROASTERS

After returning home from a lengthy stay in Indonesia, Temple founder and barista Sean Kohmescher (shown) opened the first Temple Coffee house on S Street in 2005. His dream was to create a gathering place, much like the temples he visited in his travels. His vision was simple. Good vibe, great service and exceptionally well-prepared coffee. Over the past ten years, the vision has grown to include five coffee houses and a roastery that prepares the delectable bean juice used at each Temple location and sold to restaurants around the region. The roastery holds monthly coffee education courses on home brewing, tasting and espresso preparation, and free weekly tastings. In keeping with its "Farm to Cup" sustainable coffee sourcing philosophy, Temple's Director of Coffee Eton Tsuno travels six to eight months a year to meet coffee producers and build sustainable, direct relationships with farms. Temple was named a top coffee roaster in the U.S. by CNN and *Fortune* magazine.

2200 K Street
916.662.7625

2829 S Street
916.454.1272

1010 9th Street
916.443.4960
templecoffee.com

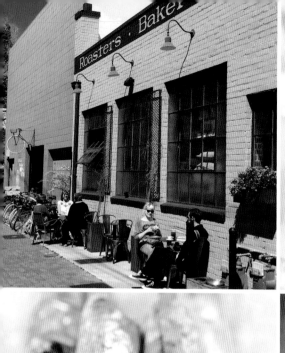

INSIDE *the Handle*

The Handle District, tucked between Downtown and Midtown, is one of the city's smaller neighborhoods.

It includes an exciting group of restaurants, bars, nightclubs and retail businesses in the area bounded by 18th and 19th Streets, L Street and Capitol Avenue. It is also home to one of the city's most visited alleys.

Interesting historic commercial buildings, restored Victorians and newly designed apartment homes sit comfortably side by side and give the neighborhood an eclectic feel on easily walkable city streets.

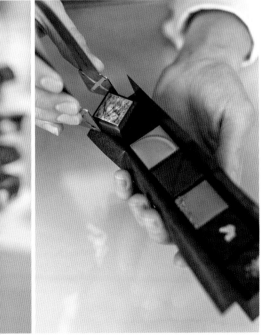

GINGER ELIZABETH CHOCOLATES

Pure bittersweet chocolate ganache. Liquid caramel punctuated by fleur de sel. Almond praline with crunchy croquant. The display cases at Ginger Elizabeth Chocolates reveal a world of sweet sophistication unmatched in Sacramento. Formally trained chocolatier and pastry chef Ginger Elizabeth Hahn and her husband, Tom (who manages the business), have created a decadent hot spot, selling delicious items made from the finest ingredients. Specializing in bon-bons, pralines, caramels, dessert bars and macarons, Ginger Elizabeth celebrates the venerable craft of chocolate guided by principles of freshness. Those principles are apparent in every bite. All products at Ginger Elizabeth are natural and contain no preservatives. The subtle sheen of the tempered chocolate is always natural, never dyed or artificially colored. The couverture chocolate is carefully culled from top-notch cacao sources. All dairy products are certified humane. And Ginger Elizabeth favors recyclable or compostable packaging made domestically. Ginger Elizabeth is chocolate at its finest.

1801 L Street, Suite 60
916.706.1738
gingerelizabeth.com

ART OF TOYS

Terri Rehg began collecting toys when she was five years old. Yet the name of her shop only hints at the depth and diversity of her remarkable talent for gathering fun and artistic treasures. Art of Toys presents a precisely edited collection of vintage toys and playthings for kids, especially around the holidays. But Rehg's real claim to fame is the stunning local and international art that fills her 425-square-foot specialty shop. Visual and tactile gifts on display at Art of Toys include remarkable paintings and art works, unusual jewelry and unique sculptures. The inventory reflects Rehg's career, which ranged from serving as a sales manager for a line of New Zealand sheepskin toys, to 14 years in the wholesale toy trade and working in sales for Disney collectibles. When Rehg served as guest curator for an art show at the California History Museum, her dream of opening a store to combine all of her interests took flight. Her extensive website and cozy shop hold endless wonders, from artwork that rotates on a regular basis to gifts and desk decorations. Rehg has a simple definition for the Art of Toys. She describes the shop's merchandise as "tchotchkes of all kinds."

1126 18th Street
916.446.0673
artoftoys.com

THE RIND

Three simple words encompass the philosophy of The Rind: "Cheese. Wine. Beer." The cheese-centric bar in the Handle District offers artisanal cheeses paired with wines and beers selected by the two certified sommeliers and one certified cicerone—beer taster—on staff. Cheese enthusiasts explore all variety of exotic cheese products, from buttery and blue to nutty and stinky—created from local dairy sources. After sampling an array of slices, customers indulge their imaginations with "grown up" versions of grilled cheese sandwiches and mac and cheese. There are special discounts for "Legen-Dairy Hour," The Rind's version of happy hour. Sara Arbabian, who co-owns the shop with her husband, beer enthusiast Steve Tatterson, has made it her mission to offer locals the experience of a farm-to-fork wine bar without all the fuss and with a focus on fresh ingredients. The result is a tribute to what it means to live and eat well in Sacramento. The Rind features homemade morabas, or preserves, in flavors such as kumquat, pear and cardamom and quince. Each jar is handmade by Sherean Arbabian, The Rind's official "Resident Chef Mother."

1801 L Street, Suite 40
916.441.7463
therindsacramento.com

MULVANEY'S BUILDING & LOAN

Patrick Mulvaney is serious when he says, "Whatever comes in the front door goes on your plate." A leader of the local farm-to-fork revolution, Mulvaney and his wife, Bobbin, built their reputations around the farm-fresh ingredients and local produce that comprise his masterful Chef's Menus. The offerings at Mulvaney's Building & Loan change daily to accommodate the harvests and the seasons. The chef's New American cuisine features complex and delectable dishes like charcuterie, seared Hudson Valley foie gras, veal sweetbread bruschetta and brace of stuffed quail. Lunch favorites include the open-faced pork scaloppini sandwich with mustard aioli and pickled vegetables. The gastronomic magic comes together in a converted 1893 firehouse. Brick walls, exposed ductwork and repurposed firehouse doors-as-windows give the restaurant a celebratory vibe that blends into a garden patio. Through the leafy adjacent courtyard stands Next Door, Mulvaney's banquet hall. Next Door features two rooms with bow truss redwood ceilings. The rooms seat 30 or 100 guests, with fine dining assured.

1215 19th Street
916.441.6022
mulvaneysbl.com

ZOCALO

Towering ceilings and expansive windows beckon natural light and make the inside and outside worlds blend seamlessly at Zocalo. Next comes the décor: mammoth urns, intricate iron works, slab tables and stunning tableware create a culturally stimulating atmosphere for the food and drinks that follow. Housed in the handsomely renovated Arnold Brothers building, which served as a Hudson car dealership in the 1920s, Zocalo's eccentric interior is inspired by the majestic town square of Mexico City, a gathering spot for centuries that embraces its past while embarking toward the future. The food is fresh and colorful, with delightful twists on Mexican menu staples such as queso fundido, empanadas, quesadillas, ceviche, enchiladas and exceptional guacamole. The Cadillac margarita is popular with the bar crowd. Zocalo's massive bar features TV monitors and romantic booths. An expansive patio completes the indoor-outdoor experiences and overlooks Capitol Avenue.

1801 Capitol Avenue
916.441.0303
zocalosacramento.com

INSIDE *Land Park*

Land Park is known for its historic homes, tree-lined streets, and vibrant City College campus life, as well as for its namesake William Land Park, Sacramento's largest urban oasis. Attractions located within the park include a golf course, the WPA Rock Garden, Fairytale Town, and a boutique zoo.

Shops and eateries are located in the vibrant Broadway District, home to the historic Tower Theater, the Old City Cemetery, Sacramento Historic Rose Garden and the original Tower Records location (now a bookstore).

Adjacent to Land Park, the Curtis Park neighborhood is an active, tight-knit community, with homes in an eclectic mix of architectural styles. South Land Park is known for its rolling hills and mid-century vibe, and Hollywood Park features affordable homes for family-oriented living.

FAIRYTALE TOWN

Humpty Dumpty's pint-sized gates welcome more than 230,000 guests each year at Fairytale Town, placing the iconic park among the region's top destinations for younger audiences. Since 1959, the Land Park play zone has stood proud and unique with its timeless blend of imaginative architecture and hands-on activities. Supported primarily by public donations and attendance, Fairytale Town builds upon its half-century of success with educational programs and literary connections to inspire new generations. Today, Fairytale Town alumni treat their grandchildren to tours of the Yellow Brick Road and the Crooked Mile. They hitch rides on Cinderella's Coach and hold court in King Arthur's Castle. The park annually welcomes guests from more than 30 California counties and provides inclusive fun for kids from every socioeconomic background and neighborhood. Free admission is provided to low-income children and disabled youngsters, ensuring a positive, enriching experience for everyone.

3901 Land Park Drive
916.808.7462
fairytaletown.org

SACRAMENTO ZOO

Nature comes alive at the Sacramento Zoo. Like its residents and guests, the zoo has evolved in purpose and stature over a history that spans 89 years. When the facility opened in 1927, its name was William Land Park Zoo. There were 40 animals, including monkeys, raccoons, birds, deer and other small animals. Today, the zoo features a menagerie of more than 500 birds, mammals and reptiles living on 14.2 acres. Emphasis is on conservation, education, appreciation and respect for these unique creatures who share our community. Among the exotics are the reticulated giraffe, Grevy's zebra, ring-tailed lemur, African lion, giant anteater and many more. The Sacramento Zoo is an oasis where guests wander shaded pathways and view nature from a perspective designed along organic, interactive lines. The zoo is the perfect location for personal meditation and youthful inspiration in the heart of the city.

3930 W. Land Park Drive
916.808.5888
saczoo.org

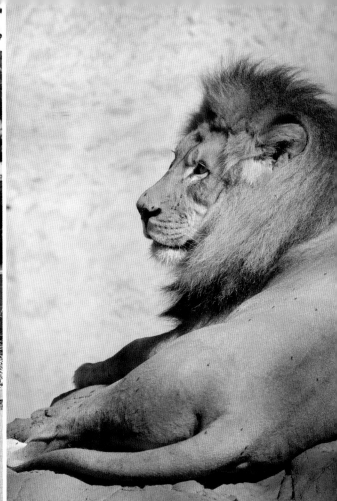

FREEPORT BAKERY

A passion for baking brought a sweet life to Marlene and Walter Goetzeler. As co-owners of Freeport Bakery for the past 28 years, the Goetzelers share a love of baking forged the first day they met. The story might have been written for Hollywood. Walter, raised by a prominent baking family in Bavaria, wandered into a San Diego bookshop run by Marlene. He was looking for a map. She wanted a German tutor. The fit was perfect. Love blossomed. Decades later, the duo dishes up incredible specialty cakes and delicious desserts—including Danish pastries, muffins, pies, cookies and savory items—from scratch at their full-line bakery with the help of 50 staff members. Freeport Bakery is an iconic Land Park location with a vintage-inspired interior detailed with as much care as the baked goods they create. Customers drive miles to retrieve custom orders. On top of all that, Marlene serves as president of the Retail Bakers of America, which offers hands-on workshops, bakery tours, educational classes, local vendor displays and annual road shows to connect baking aficionados across the country.

2966 Freeport Boulevard
916.442.4256
freeportbakery.com

RIVERSIDE CLUBHOUSE

There were no shortcuts to success in repurposing the old dive bar Hereford House on Riverside Boulevard in Land Park. The dump hadn't been updated in decades. The neglect required a massive overhaul to produce a beautiful new culinary destination. Today, the Riverside Clubhouse is the pride of Land Park, another victory for owners Matt and Fred Haines. With a menu built upon traditional American classics and a setting unrivaled, Riverside Clubhouse features a 30-foot wall of water and a three-tiered fireplace on the lovely, secluded patio. There are three 50-inch plasma TV monitors and a spectacular "burning crystal" fireplace in the lounge, which is among the most popular in town. Short ribs, cheesy grits, fish tacos and a killer Cubano sandwich provide alternatives to a classic assortment of burgers. The old Hereford cow from generations forgotten watches over the front door.

2633 Riverside Boulevard
916.448.9988
riversideclubhouse.com

123

TAYLOR'S MARKET & KITCHEN

Opened in 1962 by Roy Taylor and Ed Schell, Taylor's Market is a gem in the residential neighborhood where Land Park and Curtis Park meet. The subsequent generation of owners, Ed's son Kevin and friend Danny Johnson (hired as a butcher at age 19 in 1983) dedicated themselves to Taylor's reputation for service and quality. A remodel in 1988 brought new displays for local produce, fine wines and the best meats and seafood in town, plus partnership with local produce purveyor Aki Kushida and son Bruce, who still manages the fresh produce department. Roots run deep among the staff. Store manager Dave Hunter was 17 when he went to work at Taylor's. Meat department manager Paul Carras grew up in the neighborhood and started his career at age 15. Felicia Johnson, daughter of owners Danny and Kathy Johnson, is Taylor's cheese monger. Next door, Taylor's Kitchen features a seasonal menu created by Chef Justin Lower with a focus on fresh local foods. Desserts are created in-house. The wine list is selected by Master Sommelier candidate Keith Fergel. Part market, part fine dining, Taylor's is a Sacramento icon.

2900 & 2924 Freeport Boulevard
916.443.5154
taylorsmarket.com

HISTORIC ROSE GARDEN

History and horticulture come to life in Sacramento's Old City Cemetery. The Historic Rose Garden was founded in 1992 as a place where roses from historic locations throughout the Mother Lode and beyond could be preserved, studied and enjoyed. The garden, which reaches peak bloom in early spring, has grown to 500 old roses of various types, including plants that no longer exist elsewhere. Planted and maintained by volunteers whose efforts are led by curator Anita Clevenger, the

Historic Rose Garden and adjacent cemetery gardens demonstrate how a group of concerned citizens can transform an overrun, neglected city cemetery back into a showplace reminiscent of Victorian times. The Old City Cemetery includes perennial and native plant gardens maintained by volunteers. The Historic Rose Garden has received international honors, including the World Federation of Rose Societies' prestigious "Garden of Excellence" award. People visit from around the world to see the gardens, as well as the monuments of Sacramento pioneers at the Old City Cemetery.

1000 Broadway
oldcitycemetery.com

CASA GARDEN RESTAURANT

Very rarely can guests enjoy outstanding food in a gorgeous garden setting while contributing to a local charity. Casa Garden Restaurant provides the setting and the opportunity. Since 1973, Casa Garden and its event space, brightened by garden views from every window, have featured a rotating weekly menu created by master chefs. Specials have included sausage and ratatouille over linguine, salsa verde pork enchiladas and grilled romaine with shrimp, followed by decadent desserts like raspberry pie, caramel pecan cheesecake and strawberry margarita torte. This remarkable restaurant is run entirely by volunteers from the Los Niños Service League to raise funds for the Sacramento Children's Home, a nonprofit organization that provides life-changing programs and counseling services for children and families in need. Thanks to the amazing menus designed by the Casa Garden chefs and the tireless work of hundreds of volunteers, nearly $2.9 million has benefited the Sacramento Children's Home over the past four decades.

2760 Sutterville Road
916.452.2809
casagardenrestaurant.org

VIC'S ICE CREAM

Family owned since 1947, this Land Park heritage spot has been the site of postgame celebrations, report card rewards and summertime gab sessions for almost 70 years. Along with the traditional ice cream parlor favorites such as sundaes, shakes, cups and cones in 29 familiar flavors, Vic's offers an array of American diner classics, including corned beef, tuna and egg salad sandwiches, the Krautdog and Cheezedog and daily soup specials. The menu shifts with the seasons, but the popular dogs are always available. The Vic's experience expanded three years ago with Vic's Café, located next door to the original ice cream shop. The Café features an expanded menu with burritos, entrée salads, pulled pork sliders and baked goods, plus beer and coffee beverages, including a classic espresso. The original Vic's hasn't changed much since its grand opening in 1947 when current owner Craig Rutledge's father, Ash, and buddy Vic Zito—for whom the diner is named—banded together to open the ice cream business of their dreams. The counter stools, black-and-white checkered linoleum floor and blue jean uniforms all speak to Vic's rich history and Land Park legacy. The shop makes its specialty treats available for takeaway to parties and celebrations.

3199 Riverside Boulevard
916.448.0892
vicsicecream.com

3193 Riverside Boulevard
916.475.1223
cafevics.com

NEW HELVETIA BREWING COMPANY

Sacramento roots run deep at New Helvetia Brewing Company. Owner Dave Gull, whose Sacramento provenance dates back four generations, honored history by naming his brewery after the city's original identifier as selected in 1839 by founder John Sutter. The brewery dates from 2012, and Gull's inspiration doesn't stop at the name. He follows the brewing philosophy of the old Buffalo Brewing Company, founded in 1890 and one of the grandest beer operations west of the Mississippi from its now-forgotten sprawling headquarters at 21st and Q Streets. Gull's great-grandfather was friendly with the Buffalo Brewing Company's owners, and New Helvetia is a logical path to reclaiming a piece of Sacramento heritage. The beers, tasting room décor and even the New Helvetia building on Broadway are historic. Today, New Helvetia has become home to beer lovers on a neighborhood and national scale. The brewery won the gold medal for Historical Beer at the 2014 Great American Beer Festival, the only local brewery so honored.

1730 Broadway
916.469.9889
newhelvetiabrew.com

WILLIE'S BURGERS

Willie's is a quirky burger joint specializing in timeless classics that made drive-ins and diners famous. The menu is full of traditional favorites such as onion rings, chili cheese fries, milkshakes and big, juicy hamburgers. Owner Bill Taylor, a Land Park native and the "Willie" for whom the restaurant is named, made it his mission to offer locals a serious burger joint. The community responded by making Willie's one of the most successful burger operations in town. Taylor perfected his skills while spending time at the legendary Tommy's in Los Angeles. He took his hibachi with him wherever he went after learning to cook in the National Guard. With three locations—the original right off Broadway, a second in Arden-Arcade and a new third space in Old Sacramento headed by Taylor's son Greg and Greg's wife, Rachel Glabe Taylor—Willie's ensures there's always a burger within reach.

2415 16th Street
110 K Street
916.444.2006
williesburgers.com

IRON GRILL

Broadway and 13th Street is an unpretentious corner of the city where a simple sign beckons diners to a steakhouse mecca. The sign says "Iron." Behind the doors is a restaurant devoted to hearty eating, with emphasis on red meat traditions such as a 16-ounce New York steak or eight-ounce filet mignon. The mastermind behind Iron Grill is Bill Taylor, the founder of Willie's Burgers. Iron was originally conceived as a casual, neighborhood steakhouse but has evolved into an exceptional foodie attraction with abundant menu choices created by Chef Keith Swiryn. Bottomless mimosas and spicy Bloody Mary wake-ups enhance the breakfast experience, along with buttermilk pancakes and omelets. Iron has a full bar, which is sleek and popular with locals from nearby Land Park.

2422 13th Street
916.737.5115
irongrillsacramento.com

INSIDE *Oak Park*

The city's first suburb is a history-rich and diverse community on the rebound. Many of Oak Park's historic residences were built before World War II.

The Broadway Triangle is home to more than 40 new urban-style homes and apartments, restaurants and locally owned shops. The monthly Gather event attracts folks from all over to enjoy the neighborhood ambiance.

From the beautifully renovated McClatchy Park and Guild Theater in the 40 Acres complex to the historic properties and bike-friendly streets, this is likely the most interesting place to live, work and play in the city.

DISPLAY: CALIFORNIA

Roshaun Davis and his wife, Maritza, founded the events marketing agency Unseen Heroes to help neighborhood businesses promote events and inventories. That was 2008. Today, the mission has expanded into a creative Oak Park gathering place where local residents shop and connect with their community. Under the name DISPLAY: California, the 850-square-foot retail space provides room for revolving pop-up shops every four to eight weeks, bringing renewed energy to the emerging Triangle District. Inspired by pop-up shops in New York, Los Angeles and San Francisco, DISPLAY has one essential difference. Instead of setting up shop in a temporary space that disappears along with the inventory when the pop-up closes, the Davis family created a permanent space to house a constantly evolving concept. The shop features seasonal themes. "Holladay" was precisely that—unique holiday options from top California designers with apparel, toys, jewelry, beauty and body care products, home accessories and décor. The springtime store, "Bodega," featured artisanal food, kitchen goods and household items in a quaint general store atmosphere. Nothing is ever the same at DISPLAY: California.

3433 Broadway
916.692.5560
displaycalifornia.com

THE PLANT FOUNDRY

Oak Park might not seem an obvious location for a unique boutique that specializes in artisanal plants and flowers, but Plant Foundry Nursery & Store owner Angela Pratt is not a merchant who followed a familiar path to her success. From childhood, Pratt loved getting her hands dirty while digging in the dirt. Her mother took her to a local nursery for its calming influence and rewarded young Pratt with plants. That early exposure was never forgotten. After an education that included horticultural studies at American River College and UC Davis, Pratt's dream shop became a reality in December 2015, when she discovered the perfect Broadway location in a former filling station. The artisanal Plant Foundry specializes in edible and ornamental plants, artisan goods, organic gardening, quality tools, supplies and gifts. Driven by Pratt's dedication and deep roots in the nursery business, The Plant Foundry has blossomed.

3500 Broadway
916.917.5787
plantfoundry.com

MAKE/DO SACRAMENTO

Make/Do Sacramento may be the most unique store in Sacramento. Not merely an antiques shop, not simply a craft supply store, not just a place for vintage fabrics and handmade objects from local artists, Make/Do Sacramento is all of that and more. Opened in 2015 by Lori Easterwood, the shop is the realization of Easterwood's Tennessee provenance and exquisite taste. "Being from the South, we have a 'mend and make-do' mindset," she says. "You don't just go out and buy something new, you make it work." The dreamy Oak Park boutique is beautifully curated with vintage fabric, handmade items from local artists, craft supplies and quirky antiques. Easterwood's entrepreneurial turn was predestined. She comes from a family with a "big history of small business ownership," she says. A lifelong antique collector, she scours estate sales and tracks artists at regional craft fairs for her remarkable inventory.

2907 35th Street
makedosac.com

OAK PARK BREWING COMPANY

From an Oak Park garage, two couples pursued their love of artisanal beer and perfected their home-brewing skills. Encouraged by friends, they became confident enough to turn the passion into a profession. In 2014, Oak Park Brewing Company was founded by Shannon Karvonen, Dave Estis, Tom Karvonen, and Bonnie Peterson (shown from left to right in photo). It's a classic tale of entrepreneurial patience and faith, with no shortcuts. From its original casual brew days serving friends and a half-dozen beers on tap—easy drinking pales to stouts, sours and Belgian ales—Oak Park Brewing is a commercial success story. Housed in a 90-year-old brick building, Oak Park Brewing's award-winning beers are produced in copper-clad barrels that provide an aesthetic charm. The patio is friendly and large. And there's more than beer. The pub's creative kitchen features Irish fries with braised rabbit gravy and provolone cheese, pulled pork sliders, oven-roasted Brussels sprouts, a Cajun buttermilk shrimp po-boy, St. Louis spare ribs and a Niçoise salad. Weekend brunch finds chicken and waffles, breakfast nachos and bottomless mimosas drawing crowds.

3514 Broadway
916.660.2723
opbrewco.com

LA VENADITA

With décor inspired by the artistry of Frida Kahlo's masterpiece "The Wounded Deer," this hotspot for creative Mexican food is a homecoming for restaurateur Thomas Schnetz and his brother and business partner, David. The Schnetzes grew up in Sacramento and opened their first restaurant locally before establishing a string of successful eateries in the Bay Area. La Venadita is the Oak Park culmination of their experience, featuring the authentic cuisine Thomas learned to prepare during his frequent trips to Mexico. The menu includes simple, tasty dishes such as crispy carnitas tacos, albondigas (meatball) tacos, enchiladas with mushrooms, asparagus and poblano cream, vegetarian chile relleno and combo plate classics. La Venadita means "little deer" and the restaurant's logo derived from Kahlo's self-portrait as a deer struggling to overcome fate. A full bar highlighted by tequila and mescal libations, including specialty margaritas, piña coladas and daiquiris, keeps customers refreshed and relaxed.

3501 3rd Avenue
916.400.4676
lavenaditasac.com

OLD SOUL CO.

Serendipity describes the concept of Old Soul Co. The owners, Tim Jordan and Jason Griest (shown), first met over coffee. Jordan was one of Griest's first customers when Griest opened Naked Coffeehouse in 2002. Four years later, these two talented men formalized their ideas for artisanal breads and coffee roasting into a business partnership that advanced Sacramento's reputation as one of the best independent and craft coffee cities in the United States. Today, Old Soul Co. has four local locations, all successful and true to the spirit of fresh coffee and breads in a pleasant urban environment. The original Old Soul Co. grew from the discovery of an obscure but charming former storage warehouse in an alley near 18th and L Streets. Today, the old warehouse serves as the base of operations for the brand's roasting, baking and educational classes. Old Soul Co. sources coffee from Ethiopia, Mexico, Costa Rica, Nicaragua, Panama and Honduras. Fresh baked goods are created daily. The newest location on R Street features not only coffee, but a full-service restaurant and bar called Pullman—a salute to the historic corridor's legacy as the street where Theodore Judah engineered the West's first rail line in 1852. The bar features casual classics and craft cocktails.

The Alley
1716 L Street (rear alley)

Old Soul @ 40 Acres
3434 Broadway

Old Soul at The Weatherstone
812 21st Street

Old Soul Co. and Pullman Bar
12th and R Streets
oldsoulco.com

UNDERGROUND BOOKS & GUILD THEATER

Underground Books doesn't simply serve its neighborhood. It reflects and embraces the neighborhood—a shop that celebrates the vibrancy of Oak Park. Founded in 2003 by the gregarious Mother Rose (a.k.a. owner Georgia West), the bookstore is the community's literacy headquarters, with author talks, book discussions, children's story time sessions and countless fun events. The shop serves as an adjunct to the Guild Theater next door, which frequently showcases films, lectures and live performances. The historic Guild Theater is the only remaining theater among several early–20th century movie houses for which Oak Park was once known, and it has been noted by Sacramento author Joan Didion as the place where she enjoyed European art films as a young woman. The Guild and Underground Books are integrated within the 23,000-square-foot 40 Acres Art Gallery and Cultural Center, which houses Old Soul Co. coffeehouse, apartments and rotating exhibitions that feature student and professional artists while chronicling Oak Park's history as the city's cultural hub.

2814 35th Street
916.737.3333
underground-books.com

2828 35th Street
916.842.4906
guildtheater.com

VIBE HEALTH BAR

Clean, lean and healthy snacks are the point at Vibe Health Bar. Open since March 2016, Vibe's goal is to bring healthy food and drink options to the heart of the Broadway Triangle neighborhood in Oak Park. Açai bowls are one specialty: "superfood" açai berries mixed with organic ingredients such as coconut, local honey, granola, pineapple and bee pollen. Vibe features salads, sandwiches, wraps and unique smoothies. Notable is the "City of Trees," a blend of kale, pineapple, mango, jalapeño, basil, goji berry, ginger, coconut water and Himalayan salt, which Vibe owner

Brandon Brodzky (shown behind bar) insists "tastes like sunshine." Brodzky and his business partner Blake Houston (at left in photo) have redesigned the space to feel cozy like a coffee shop, with free Wifi and room to relax. A mini art gallery featuring local artists enhances the walls. Vibe carries products from local purveyors, including Chocolate Fish Coffee, Brass Clover Cold Brew Coffee, Revive Kombucha and Zeal Kombucha, giving customers easy access to local, healthy food and drinks.

3515 Broadway
916.382.9723
vibehealthbar.com

INSIDE *East Sac*

Cool boutiques, fabulous eateries and craft coffeehouses and brew pubs encourage get-togethers in this close-knit community.

Hike and bike the American River Parkway trail that borders family friendly, mid-century River Park. Sac State's campus brings student energy spilling over into the city's original East Sac "Little Italy" enclave.

Stroll the leafy canopied streets of the Fab Forties and Elmhurst Parkway and visit McKinley Park's public rose garden. East Sac was President Ronald Reagan's home base when he was the state's governor.

Tahoe Park features affordable housing, a budding retail scene and active families.

33RD STREET BISTRO

Food inspired by the Pacific Northwest was a unique and winning restaurant concept in 1995, when brothers Fred (shown at left) and Matt Haines returned home to Sacramento from Portland and Seattle and opened the 33rd Street Bistro. Two decades later, the brothers and their celebrated formula for success have gained iconic status in East Sacramento, where 33rd Street Bistro has established itself with extraordinary style, flavor and consistency. The sophisticated but casual eatery serves breakfast, lunch and dinner—along with a traditional happy hour that fills the bar and patio. The menu features fresh ingredients, generous portions and colorful presentations. Craft cocktails are a house specialty, and the wine list brings unique pairings with more than 40 wines from Washington, Oregon and California, all available by the glass. The Haines brothers have expanded their dining empire to include the Riverside Clubhouse in Land Park and Suzie Burger in Midtown. Their fine touch at 33rd Street Bistro remains true to the core.

3301 Folsom Boulevard
916.455.2233
33rdstreetbistro.com

CHOCOLATE FISH COFFEE ROASTERS

Small-batch coffees brewed from beans harvested within the past 12 months are the rule at Chocolate Fish Coffee Roasters, where the bean is king. Founded in 2008 by husband and wife Andy and Edie Baker, Chocolate Fish Coffee takes its product to extremes. The Bakers and their coffee-loving team travel the world to bring the best beans back to Sacramento. Among the regular stops are Guatemala, Colombia, Costa Rica, Honduras and El Salvador. On the road, the Chocolate Fish crew builds personal relationships and tracks the integrity and sustainable farming practices of purveyors. The coffee beans that find their way to Sacramento have passed inspection for microclimates, quality assurance and care in handling. The Bakers even created Specialty Coffee Week to introduce more unique flavors. A "chocolate fish" is a New Zealand confection given as thanks for a good deed. The name reflects the result at Chocolate Fish Coffee Roasters.

East Sacramento Café & Roastery
4749 Folsom Boulevard
916.451.5181

Downtown Coffee Bar
3rd and Q Streets
chocolatefishcoffee.com

CORTI BROTHERS

Brothers Frank and Gino Corti opened their grocery store in 1947 to expand the culinary experiences of Sacramento residents. They offered delicacies and wines from around the world, not easily available in Northern California at the time. Frank's son, Darrell Corti (shown), continues the tradition in the quaint East Sacramento grocery store. Darrell's encyclopedic knowledge of food and wine led to the creation in 1967 of his legendary food newsletter, featuring products discovered on travels abroad. The letter is still published to ravenous readers across the country. Corti was knighted as a Cavaliere by the Italian government for his work in promoting Italian products. Today, America's top chefs seek his opinion on all matters culinary. The Corti team includes expert wine stewards and journeyman meat cutters, but the store retains the old-fashioned charm first envisioned by the Corti brothers. The full-service delicatessen is famous for sandwiches and ravioli, the oldest continuously produced food product in Sacramento. The selection of charcuterie and cheese is comprehensive, as is the stock of specialty food products from all over the world.

5810 Folsom Boulevard
916.736.3800
cortibrothers.com

EAST SAC HARDWARE

Sheree Johnston is called "The Hardware Lady." Equal parts teacher, problem solver, business manager and team leader, Johnston owns East Sac Hardware with her husband, Rich (she is shown here with their son, Ricky). Sheree holds a master's degree in education and ran the local, independent hardware store's paint department in the late 1980s and early 1990s, so she's well qualified for her multiple tasks. The shop has served East Sacramento and the surrounding area since 1951 and features the essentials—tools, fasteners, plants, plumbing supplies, key cutting, tool sharpening, screen and lamp repair services and, naturally, paint—with a focus on products made in the U.S. The Hardware Lady conducts classes on the Amy Howard At Home One Step Paint system, antiquing, household repairs and general strategies for hands-on home improvement.

4800 Folsom Boulevard
916.457.7558
eastsachardware.com

159

OPA! OPA!

Phil Courey was raised on the classic Mediterranean dishes he features in his lively and colorful East Sacramento neighborhood restaurant. Opa! Opa! delivers the spirit, variety and freshness of Greek dining with dishes that highlight roasted lamb and marinated chicken, yogurt, spinach, cucumbers, olives and feta cheese. House specialties include spanakopita with feta and spinach, and dolmathes—the delicacy of stuffed grape leaves ubiquitous in the Mediterranean. Another traditional Greek favorite is gyro—spiced and tender, with a dip of tzatziki, carved from a cone of beef and lamb. The restaurant has a companion dessert shop called Sweeties, where classic baklava is served along with cupcakes, bars and cappuccinos.

5644 J Street
916.451.4000
eatatopa.com

160

CABANA WINERY

A small but mighty tasting room in the heart of East Sacramento brings the wine universe to the capital. After 17 years of producing award-winning wine in the foothills, owner Robert Smerling decided to move his operation into the city. He opened an urban winery with an impressive wine list that encourages repeat inspection. Eight wines are created specifically for the Cabana Wines label. Additional options include whites, reds, sweet wines and ports from Napa, Lodi and further afield, including France, Italy, Spain and Argentina. The wines are paired with a carefully edited selection of food. Traditional charcuterie and artisanal cheese plates complete the experience in the tasting room. Salads, hearty entrées such as risotto and spaghetti and meatballs and wood-fired pizzas are available. In another nice touch, guests' dogs are welcome on the patio. Visits become family affairs.

5610 Elvas Avenue
916.476.5492
cabanawinery.com

FORMOLI'S BISTRO

They dreamed of opening a boutique restaurant specializing in eclectic European food and succeeded beyond expectations. The husband and wife team of Aimal Formoli and Suzanne Ricci draw their inspiration primarily from France, Spain and Italy for the bistro's perpetually evolving dishes. Chef Formoli trained at the California Culinary Academy. His menu reflects a global vision but source materials come from close to home, with meat and vegetables provided by regional farmers and ranchers. Favorites include Medjool dates stuffed with goat cheese, ground lamb sliders and a cast-iron fennel pot—a delicious combination of braised fennel, onions, breadcrumbs, Grana Padano, Swiss cheese and herbs with house-made bread. Another house specialty is the decadent whiskey burger, with Five Dot Ranch beef. At the bar, local residents gather over selections from Formoli's extensive wine list. The interior is a mix of European style and flair. Paintings literally lean off the walls, which are painted a rich eggplant hue. In warm weather, the energy gravitates to the front patio, which overlooks J Street.

3839 J Street
916.448.5699
formolisbistro.com

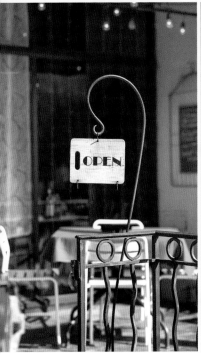

formoli's
an east sacramento **BISTRO**

KATIA'S COLLECTIONS

Three rules prevail at Katia's Collections. The garment must feel good to the touch. It must be of the highest quality and comfortable to wear. And the fit and color must be right. The selection process becomes a pleasure under the guidance of Paris native Katia Kemmler, who brings her unique French aesthetic and considerable experience to every client she dresses. Although she's lived in the U.S. for more than three decades, she remains determined to honor French styling while never being predictable yet always chic. Kemmler helps customers identify pieces that beautifully fulfill the three criteria while staying within budget. With administrative support from Kemmler's husband, Richard, Katia's Collections serves a diverse spectrum of clients and donates to local organizations through fundraising fashion shows.

5619 H Street
916.451.8966
katiascollections.com

KERRIE KELLY DESIGN LAB

Interior designer and author Kerrie Kelly travels the world to discover the latest inspirations in sleek, approachable design. Her journeys reaffirm Kelly's belief that every home or workplace deserves a beautiful look, which reflects the mantra of her interior design business and East Sac design lab. An award-winning and certified interior designer with 20 years in the business and experience at every level, large and small, Kelly brings a precise, appropriate touch to any commercial or residential space. She specializes in bright, comfortable designs that aren't intimidated by luxury or beholden to trends. Kelly accommodates a variety of styles and preferences, from organic luxury living to reimagined classic designs brought to life with texture, color and light. In addition to helping Sacramento home and business owners achieve their dream interiors, Kelly judges student design competitions and launches product collaborations with international kitchen and bath companies. And she's a multimedia consultant for several national home furnishing brands. The Kerrie Kelly Design Lab offers retail accessories with a specialty in window coverings. The lab features more than 150 window treatment styles, all custom-made in the United States.

5704 Elvas Avenue
916.706.2089
kerriekelly.com

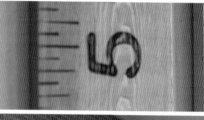

KOUKLA KIDS

Fun, funky and functional apparel, plus accessories and gifts for newborns up to kids' size 8—Koukla Kids boutique for children is Sacramento's one-stop shop for the stylish youngster and parent. The tiny store, owned by Toria Kaufman, Kristen Kinter and Amy Schnetz (shown left to right) is packed with chic clothing and gear for active peewees. An internationally inspired inventory features designer lines such as Scout, with its high-quality organic cotton, and 3 Pommes, a favorite of European babies. Ultra-chic children will love Petit Bateau, a French company that specializes in soft cotton loungewear and undergarments. And there's Little Maven, which features boys wear designed by Tori Spelling. The unique collections change with the seasons but always stay a step or two ahead of trends. The shop also carries cute handmade hair accessories, books and gifts from Pylones, Barefoot, Eboo and Green. Koukla Kids is the place where every parent and youngster can find the top new lines from Europe and beyond.

3809 J Street
916.254.5437
kouklakids.com

McKINLEY PARK CENTER

Wedding receptions, parties and smaller gatherings find an elegant home in the Art Deco-era Grand Hall at East Sacramento's historic McKinley Park. With lovingly restored wood paneling and timber beams, the Grand Hall provides an inspirational setting for any event. The building and grounds are part of the Clunie Community Center, an updated 1930s facility run by the nonprofit Friends of East Sacramento. The center features four unique rental spaces for groups of 12 to 200 people, including kitchen facilities and a patio overlooking the park and swimming pool. A smaller rental room features an historic display of East Sacramento photographs. Friends of East Sacramento also manages the breathtakingly beautiful McKinley Rose Garden, the city's best, with 1,200 rose bushes, eight companion perennial beds and a wrought iron gazebo. Rental rates are very affordable at this popular venue, maintained by a group of dedicated volunteers who keep the gardens perfectly manicured within the timeless and historic setting.

Alhambra Boulevard and H Street
916.243.8292
mckinleyparkcenter.org

3033 - Scene in McKinley Park, Sacramento, California.

ONESPEED

Sausage, tomatoes, potatoes, caramelized onions, olives and goat cheese provide essential sustenance at OneSpeed, a self-described "neighborhood pizza joint" whose ambition belies the name. Opened in 2009 and crafted around a bicycle theme, OneSpeed is a casual but sophisticated counterpoint to owner Rick Mahan's superb Midtown restaurant, The Waterboy. OneSpeed celebrates fresh and locally sourced ingredients and conjures simple flavors from dishes Mahan calls "seasonally relevant." The pizzas are a joy, from the healthy garden pie to the meaty sausage pie. Options run deep at OneSpeed. Antipasto and spaghetti pomodoro represent classic fare. There's even a burger, with a homemade bun stacked high with sautéed onions, peppers, white cheddar and rosemary mayonnaise.

4818 Folsom Boulevard
916.706.1748
onespeedpizza.com

THE PINK HOUSE

How this business got its name is no secret. Look at the enticing pink bungalow and the answer is instantly revealed. Inside, the inventory delivers perpetual flirty fun. Owner Peggy Orr carefully selects the shoes, handbags, gifts and accessories. The sitting room atmosphere of The Pink House encourages gentle conversation and the experience of hands-on shopping from niche and mainstream brands such as Off the Beaten Track, Sacha London, Chocolate Blu and Franco Sarto (and that's just some of the shoe selection). Orr stocks unique accessories difficult to find elsewhere in the region. And she sources locally, highlighting designers such as Ada's Argentinian leather and gold-plated jewelry. Affordable finds can be found from Sweet Lola, plus tribal tidbits from the Bali Queen and Samoe Style, a handbag brand designed and crafted by a Colorado family with a devoted customer base that awaits each season's new releases. For all its charm, The Pink House is available for exclusive private shopping and event rental, including birthdays and bachelorette parties.

1462 33rd Street
916.737.7465

THE KITCHEN RESTAURANT

For 25 years, The Kitchen has been the ultimate dining destination for the Sacramento region and beyond. Innovative and unmatched for pure culinary enjoyment and genuine hospitality, The Kitchen serves a five-course prix fixe seasonal dinner menu featuring the best and freshest ingredients available, mostly procured locally and regionally. The executive chef and staff present the menu in a lively, theatrical demonstration format. Guests are invited to stroll throughout the open kitchen, chat with the chefs, visit the wine cellar and relax on the patio. Husband-and-wife chefs Randall Selland and Nancy Zimmer, along with their grown children, Josh Nelson and Tamera Baker, founded The Kitchen Restaurant in 1991. The Selland family was among the first to emphasize farm-to-fork dining in the Sacramento region. The quality, commitment, and passion that the Selland family brings to The Kitchen have created a landmark restaurant that has sold out nightly since its inception. The Kitchen Restaurant has earned every imaginable local and regional award along with an impressive list of national accolades, including the AAA Five Diamond Award six years running, a nod as a semi-finalist for the James Beard "Outstanding Restaurant" Award, the highest Zagat ratings, and honors from *Wine Spectator* and *Wine Enthusiast*, as well as inclusion in the Yelp Top 100 and the Open Table Top 100.

2225 Hurley Way
916.568.7171
thekitchenrestaurant.com

TWIGGS FLORAL DESIGN

Twiggs is not an average florist. As an international buyer and award-winning floral designer, owner Wes Green travels the world to gather ideas and inspiration for his unique floral creations and home accessories. Twiggs Floral Design specializes in breathtaking arrangements for any occasion for individual or corporate clients. Green and his design team hand-select and import fresh, premium flowers and botanicals daily. Arrangements demonstrate a variety of creative floral design styles to emphasize complementary or monochromatic color palettes, natural elements, plus multiple textures and botanical groupings. The Twiggs signature style follows the European aesthetic: clean, elemental and architectural, with a combination of function, fashion and form. Stunning plantscapes are the result. The tiny storefront tucked into a cluster of shops bursts with elegant décor items, glassware, candles and flora and gives Twiggs Floral Design the appearance of an enchanted apothecary brimming with nature's bounty.

3250 J Street
916.441.2302
twiggsfloraldesign.com

178

TWIGGS
Our Menu

Vased
Dozen Roses -
½ dozen Roses -
European -
Arrangement -

Hand Wrapped
Dozen Roses -
½ dozen Roses -
Single Rose -

S. BENSON & CO.

Luxurious merino wool sweaters, soft-structured European jackets and socks with whimsical patterns and wild color schemes establish the tone and deliver the style at S. Benson & Co., Sacramento's premier clothier for gentlemen. Dressing the region's male style leaders since 1995, owner Steve Benson has refined the art of shopping for gentlemen's clothes. He's transformed the retail experience into a visit to a friendly private club. Benson says his mission is to "help gentlemen define their clothing needs and provide them with garments that better reflect their personality and lifestyle, all in a comfortable and relaxed environment." Stylish and classy ready-to-wear pieces for work, weekend and evening are highlighted in the shop, but Benson also fits clients with bespoke suits made to measure. S. Benson & Co. can streamline and update any man's closet.

5617 H Street
916.452.4288
sbensonandco.com

SELLAND'S MARKET-CAFÉ

Selland's Market-Café is a casual, family-friendly neighborhood café in East Sac preparing handcrafted, quality seasonal foods. Selland's offers a wide array of menu options including wood-fired pizzas, sandwiches, fresh salads, hot and cold prepared foods from the deli cases, soups, seasonal specials and house-made desserts. At Selland's, guests can enjoy boutique and local wines by the glass and bottle, as well as craft beers and kombucha on tap. Selland's is a neighborhood institution with something for everyone. Established in 2001, Selland's Market-Café is family owned and operated by Selland Family Restaurants co-founders, chefs Randall Selland and Nancy Zimmer and their grown children, Josh Nelson and Tamera Baker. A second location in Land Park will open in late 2016. The Selland family also owns acclaimed local restaurants The Kitchen, Ella Dining Room & Bar and OBO' Italian Table and Bar. The Selland family has provided high-quality dining experiences using products and ingredients sourced largely from local producers and the area's farmers markets for 25 years.

5340 H Street
916.736.3333

915 Broadway
sellands.com

KRU

Raw and refined, traditional and innovative, an inspired fusion of Asian, European and American ingredients and cooking techniques—such is the daily routine at Kru Contemporary Japanese Cuisine. Owner and chef Buu "Billy" Ngo (shown in hat) is the creative guide behind Kru's visually stunning and delicious dishes. He's a foodie celebrity, with appearances on culinary TV shows such as "Glutton for Punishment," "Man Fire Food" and "Cutthroat Kitchen." The chef was born in Hong Kong and moved to Sacramento as a baby. Kru started small, but today the restaurant is celebrated as the city's chicest sushi provider, with plates that please eye and palate. The menu features traditional classics, including wakame (seaweed) salad, house-made pork gyoza, shrimp and vegetable tempura, chicken teriyaki, and pork belly and sea urchin uni served with teriyaki, arare and chili oil powder. Kru—the name is derived from the French word *cru*, or raw—also specializes in classics such as hamachi carpaccio, nigiri, sashimi and an array of sushi and hand rolls almost too beautiful to eat.

3145 Folsom Boulevard
916.551.1559
krurestaurant.com

57TH STREET ANTIQUE & DESIGN CENTER

A mixture of sophisticated interior and exterior furnishings and design, food, spa services and antiques beckons at 57th Street Antique & Design Center. Called "the best-kept secret in Sacramento" by owner Gary Little, the 40,000-square-foot, multi-building historic complex near Elvas Avenue between H and J Streets has established itself among the city's most eclectic centers, offering an acre of parking. Today the center includes retail gift and curated antique shops, full-service interior designers, a cross-training gym, a salon and spa and an award-winning family restaurant run by chef Evan Elsberry. Evan's Kitchen and Catering is open for all three meals Tuesday through Saturday and for

breakfast and lunch on Sundays. The popular eatery also offers notable winemaker dinners throughout the year. Stunning specialty shops showcasing original home designs and emerging décor trends mingle with antique shops of exceptional quality and style. Spend an hour or an entire day exploring the center's many treasures and experiences.

855 57th Street
57thstreetantiquerow.com

NOPALITOS SOUTHWESTERN CAFÉ

Southwestern cooking is a savory family affair at Nopalitos Southwestern Café, where husband and wife owners Dave and Rose Hanke share duties in the kitchen and front of the house. Opened in 1992 and packed with customers ever since, Nopalitos takes its name from the nopal cactus, a staple in Mexican kitchens beloved for its versatility and light, tangy flavor. The Hankes are masters of nopal cooking and coax delicious, understated magic from the edible, elongated cactus pads. Dave typically works the stove, while Rose bakes, serves dishes and maintains the restaurant's books. Nopalitos devotees arrive early for chile verde, chile colorado, smothered burrito, vegetarian Nopalitos quesadilla with roasted poblano chilies, along with traditional tamales, tostadas and tacos. As befits its home-style provenance, Nopalitos maintains quirky hours—the doors are open only for breakfast and lunch, and the kitchen closes on weekends.

5530 H Street
916.452.8226
nopalitoscafe.com

BACON & BUTTER

Immensely popular for breakfast, brunch and lunch, Bacon & Butter opened in Midtown in 2012 and relocated to Tahoe Park in 2014. The restaurant provides a classic study of farm-to-fork done right. Lines form around 8 A.M. for locally sourced meals created by chef and owner Billy Zoellin, who was raised nearby in Tahoe Park. Menus include bananas foster French toast, biscuits and bacon gravy, mustard-roasted Brussels sprouts served with lardon and poached egg and bacon and egg flapjacks. The lunch menu features an extensive list of brews and other spirits and one of the best burgers in town, created with Storm Hill beef with bacon, Petaluma jack cheese, shallot rings and smoked aioli. Another favorite is the schnitzel sandwich, with a Niman pork cutlet served over mustard slaw on a brioche bun. The most popular drink is Zoellin's famed Bloody Mary, which is part of the breakfast and brunch tradition at Bacon & Butter.

5913 Broadway
916.346.4445
baconandbuttersac.com

191

BROWN HOUSE ON H

Take a seat on the black-and-white-striped divan and become immersed in the timelessly fashionable world of Doris Pittell. The proprietress of Brown House is an expert in chic and classic merchandise for women who want to look fabulous at every age and stage of their lives. The high-end pieces of Brown House speak to customers who know their goal: to look as stylish in a gorgeous gown or sequined jacket as they do while meeting friends for coffee in a Chanel-inspired tweed jacket and beautifully tailored slacks. Brown House has earned its niche among local residents who love brands that change with the season and work perfectly with a tightly edited accessory selection. Pittell has been in business for almost four decades. She makes the Brown House atmosphere warm and welcoming and encourages clients to lounge in the delightful sitting room and peruse fashion magazines while she buzzes around and pulls the perfect garments. Brown House specializes in clothes and accessories that make clients look great for years to come.

5379 H Street
916.973.1693

HAWKS PROVISIONS & PUBLIC HOUSE

White subway tiles, gleaming glass and chrome, warm woods, deep teal walls and bar stools that look like vintage office chairs introduce a European flair to Alhambra Boulevard in the newest restaurant project from Molly Hawks and Michael Fagnoni. Acclaimed for Hawks, their fine-dining flagship in Granite Bay, the wife and husband team has taken a more informal approach to their urban destination. Public House features a menu filled with the best ingredients from small farms and local purveyors. Familiar classics get special treatment at Public House. The burger is made with house-ground Wagyu beef. Spaghetti becomes a delicacy with slow-roasted mushrooms. And the country paté with Armagnac-soaked prunes is a delicious twist on simplicity. Next door, Provisions provides take-out options, with house-made pastries, quiche and croque monsieur sandwiches, along with daily sandwich specials. Public House fulfills the expectations of its name with a full bar, where customers enjoy craft cocktails, local beer and a convivial environment.

1525 Alhambra Boulevard
916.588.4440
hawkspublichouse.com

LES BAUX BAKERY

A taste of Paris on Folsom Boulevard blossoms at Les Baux Bakery, where French bistro–inspired meals, pastries and baguettes are made fresh in-house every day. Breakfast options include Parisian-style light croissants and hearty breakfast focaccia, as well as made-to-order coffee drinks. Hot and cold sandwiches, salads and house-made soups attract crowds at lunch, and bistro dinner mainstays such as steak and frites, moules frites and the Les Baux burger help wind down the evening. Les Baux also features Vietnamese classics, including green curry and a Vietnamese crepe made with turmeric-infused rice batter. This food fusion reflects the creative diversity of owner Trong Nguyen. Nguyen and his co-owner wife, Annie Ngo, are the talents behind the popular regional chain La Bou.

5090 Folsom Boulevard
916.739.1348
lesbauxbakery.com

V. MILLER MEATS

Traditional butcher shops are rare finds, but a shop that specializes in 100 percent whole-animal butchering is unique— which makes V. Miller Meats a remarkable homage to the meat cutter's art. Owner and butcher Eric Veldman Miller became interested in the craft of whole-animal butchery while apprenticing under Master Butcher Terry Regassa. Previously, Miller built his culinary reputation as a chef at fine dining restaurants across the region, including Mulvaney's Building & Loan in Midtown. Recognizing the connections among local farmers, natural pastures and animal welfare as integral parts of the butchering process, Miller elected to operate a craft butchery and carry only high-quality, pasture-raised and grass-fed meats. The V. Miller cold case contains pasture-raised beef, pork and lamb, free-range chicken, fresh sausage, cured meats and charcuterie, plus delectable deli meats, bone broth and stock. Head butcher Cindy Garcia makes an art of trimming the perfect cuts.

4801 Folsom Boulevard, Suite 2
916.400.4127
vmillermeats.com

AFTERWORD

Inside Sacramento reflects the neighborhoods I know best after more than 20 years of having published monthly neighborhood newsmagazines in this city. I love my adopted hometown, and I wanted others to see this beautiful, exciting city through my eyes. I am forever grateful for the entrepreneurs and small-business owners who contribute to these neighborhoods daily through their energy, drive, attention to detail and willingness to take huge risks. Together, they have helped build a unique, diverse and exciting city.

Compiling a list of the 101 most interesting places was daunting, especially in a city whose neighborhoods are constantly evolving. Each week, as we inched closer to our deadline, we found new options to consider. If we had gone to print a month later, we could have easily included a dozen or more sites.

There are a substantial number of compelling places in the city that are located beyond our selected neighborhoods. We found other businesses that we loved but that didn't work well for the book's photo format. And, unfortunately, a handful of great places that we wanted to include were not available for photography for a variety of reasons.

Finally, please know that this book is a snapshot of information on the day we went to press. Please visit insidesacbook.com and the individual business websites for updates.

—Cecily Hastings

EXPERIENCE DIGITAL @INSIDESACBOOK

While researching this book, I started using the photo-sharing app Instagram. It enables users to share photos and very short videos through the app and other social networks. Many of the places in this book share photos publicly on Instagram. If you haven't done so before, I encourage you to join and follow these great places in the digital world. (This book is also on Instagram along with our photographers: @anikophotos and @rachelvalley.)

Through Instagram, I discovered accounts that feature beautiful—sometimes breathtaking—photographs of our city. My favorites include @sacfarm2fork, @igerssac, @sacramento365, @sacafterdark, @experiencesacramento, @downtownsac, @visitsacramento, @sacitecture, @dailyflourish, @urbanfarmstead, @oldsac and @midtownfarmersmarket. Accounts like these occasionally allow guest "grammers," as they are called, to take over and post their own photos for a few days. If you like their work, you can follow them. You can also share your own shots with other users on these accounts.

Any posted photos can be categorized with tags such as #downtownsac, #visitsacramento, #crockerart, #exploremidtown and #oldsac that let you search for photos of specific places or themes. There are more than 150,000 user-generated images posted on #visitsacramento.

You can also create your own explorations of downtown Sacramento using an app called In the Sac, developed by my friend Jessica Kriegel. Using your particular interests, it helps you plan city journeys of discovery, with recommendations from knowledgeable locals. Eat Shop Play Sacramento is another good app to consider when exploring the city.

If you've never considered this digital approach, it's time to start exploring Sacramento in a completely new way!

The collage of photos and details (on right) were all featured on Instagram. Photo credits (clockwise from top left): @goodthompson, @thadtphotography, @nateecklerphotography, @claytonblakley, @steveharriman.

Instagrammers also were chosen for several of the photos on our neighborhood introduction pages. On the Old Sac introduction page, the Tower Bridge photo was by Steve Harriman. He also contributed the Tower Theater photo on the Land Park introduction page and the leafy street photo and the cycle racers on the East Sac introduction page. On the same page, Nick Anaya shot the underside of the Guy West Bridge at Sac State, and Miles McCormack shot the alley with the bicycle. The food board was shot by Bella Karragiannidis. The balance of the shots were taken by Aniko Kiezel and Rachel Valley.

Other photo credits include the Historic Rose Garden page with the top middle photo by Dean Sonneborn, bottom left photo by Miranda Saake, and bottom right photo by Debby Sprigg. On the McKinley Park Center pages, the bottom left photo is by Mary Gray and the bottom right photo is by Shay Pang. All were honored winners in the McKinley Rose Garden's annual photo contest.

INDEX OF PLACES

Photographer Key:

AK – Aniko Kiezel

RV – Rachel Valley

LS – Linda Smolek

Unmarked places are photo collaborations

ACKNOWLEDGMENTS

Creating a book like this takes a very talented team. I am blessed to have one. The fabulous work of our photographers, Aniko Kiezel and Rachel Valley, speaks for itself on every page. Jessica Laskey wrote the book and managed the relationships with participants.

Graphic designer Brian Burch helped guide me in creating this beautiful book design. Longtime book publisher Helen Sweetland, now of Left Coast Book Works here in Sacramento, was invaluable in helping me negotiate the world of book publishing, printing and distribution. And I am grateful to Bob Graswich for contributing his expert editing skills.

My husband, Jim, deserves a great deal of love and credit for keeping our business and home life running smoothly while I took nearly a year away from both to create this book. And I am very grateful to my publication staff members Daniel Nardinelli, Cindy Fuller, Michael McFarland, Marybeth Bizjak, Linda Smolek, Lisa Schmidt and Lauren Hastings, who contributed design, photography, editing, distributing or web skills.

Much appreciation goes to Melissa Davis and Kristen Loken, who published *This Is Oakland*, the guide book that was a major inspiration for our efforts.

I am grateful to the small-business owners who welcomed us into their places, shared their stories with us and helped us with book sales. They truly inspire.

I also want to thank the generous sponsors who covered a portion of the costs of producing such a high-quality and visually compelling book:

Sacramento Convention & Visitors Bureau
Fulcrum Property

Downtown Sacramento Partnership
Dunnigan Realtors
East Sacramento Chamber of Commerce
McKinley Village by The New Home Company
Midtown Business Association
Oak Park Business Association
Old Sacramento Business Association
Sacramento Metro Chamber of Commerce
Sacramento Natural Foods Co-op
Sutter District
Mayor-elect Darrell Steinberg

City Council Member Jeff Harris
City Council Member Steve Hansen
Diepenbrock Elkin Gleason LLP
Marcy Friedman
MMS Strategies
River City Bank
Sacramento State University
Tina Thomas